Terrorism, Extremism, and Islam

Adeel Zeerak

Adeel Zeerak

ISBN: 1984210831
ISBN 13: 978-1984210838
CreateSpace Independent Publishing Platform
North Charleston, South Carolina, USA

DEDICATION

This book is dedicated to every victim of terrorism, from whichever part of the world, belonging to any religion or school of thought.

ACKNOWLEDGEMENTS

I am thankful to all those who have helped or guided me in any manner in the writing or publishing of this book. Notably, Mufti Nazeer Ahmed (Advocate) and my colleague Mr. Laiq-ur-Rehman.

My father, Abdul Hafeez Qureshi (late), who played a great role in my upbringing and education.

My mother, Raisa Khanam Nighat, whose prayers, guidance, and encouragement have given me the strength to pursue my endeavors.

My other family members including my wife, Dr. Zunairah Rais, and my two wonderful kids, Ahmed Zeerak Qureshi and Muhammad Zeerak Qureshi, who are always a source of inspiration for me.

I want to convey my special thanks to my niece, Ms. Ayesha Qureshi, for sparing her valuable time for the review and editing of this entire book before publishing.

May Allah (s.w.t.) reward all of them with His blessings and mercy in this world and the Hereafter.

Adeel Zeerak

TABLE OF CONTENTS

FOREWORD

With the name of Allah, the All-Merciful, the Very-Merciful.

The post 9/11 world is very different from what it used to be. Although terrorism has a long history, it has assumed an unprecedented position in general public consciousness and discourse since the 9/11 terrorist attack in the USA. Since then, there has been an ongoing war against terrorism launched by the US and its allies in which countries like Afghanistan and Iraq were invaded. Despite this, terrorism is far from over yet. Not only are the US and other Western countries still being targeted, but various Muslim countries are also repeated victims of terrorist attacks. Beyond this, some countries also harbor terrorist activities in enemy states to fulfill their geo-political goals through asymmetric warfare. Thus, many countries including my own country, Pakistan, have paid a heavy price in their fight against terrorism both in terms of monetary losses and, more importantly, the loss of human life.

The rise of various Muslim terrorist organizations and their instigation of terrorist activities has brought a bad name to the religion of Islam. The use of the term 'Jihad' by these groups in executing their violent activities against civilian targets has raised serious doubts about the Islamic concept of Jihad. Moreover, both Muslim terrorists and non-Muslim critics of Islam have misquoted the sacred verses of the Holy Quran to prove their erroneous points of view. I therefore feel that it is necessary to analyze the concept of terrorism from an Islamic perspective and to provide the general public with the true concept of Jihad in Islam.

Striving or fighting against terrorism to free the world of this evil is imperative. The purpose of this book is to serve this goal as well.

Meanwhile, it is also important to note that during the 'war on terror', the false assertion by the US and its allies regarding the presence of weapons of mass destruction in Iraq has raised a lot of questions regarding the ongoing war. The result of this war has been tremendous human suffering in which thousands have lost their lives, been maimed, or displaced from their homelands.

I have been thinking of writing my third book based on the topic of terrorism for a long time. But due to a busy work schedule and family engagements, I was unable to accomplish this desired undertaking. This year, I have managed to find some free time to write this book addressing this extremely sensitive topic which is now available to you. This book is not a book on Islam, rather it is a book on terrorism and extremism. However, a significant portion of this book is dedicated to the teachings of Islam as there has been a rise in the phenomenon of so-called Muslim extremism in the post 9/11 world.

While writing this book, I have tried my best to present an unbiased view of the topic and use only reliable sources of information. The sacred verses of the Holy Quran, references of the current political situation in the world, records of various terrorist incidents, news articles, and Muslim historical accounts have all been cited in this book. I hope this book provides you with valuable information to comprehend the topic of extremism and terrorism and to clarify various Islamic concepts like Jihad and the treatment of non-Muslims. It is my hope that this book will also serve as a valuable resource for students and scholars alike in their research works.

Adeel Zeerak

LIST OF ABBREVIATIONS

AD   A.D. stands for Anno Domini, which is Latin for "year of our Lord," and it means the number of years since the birth of Jesus Christ.

AOG   Army of God

AQI   Al-Qaida in Iraq

AS   'alayh-i-salam' which means "Peace be upon him". This expression follows after naming any prophet other than Muhammad, or one of the archangels (i.e Gabriel, Michael, etc.)

BLA   Baluchistan Liberation Army

CE   Common Era or Current Era is a name for a calendar era widely used around the world today.

CIA   Central Intelligence Agency. US intelligence agency.

ETA   Euskadi Ta Askatasuna

FBI   Federal Bureau of Investigation

FGCM   Field General Court Martial

GOP   Grand Old Party. The Republican Party of USA.

ISI   Inter-Services Intelligence. A Pakistani intelligence agency.

ISIL   Islamic State of Iraq and the Levant

ISIS   Islamic State of Iraq and Syria

ISPR   Inter Services Public Relations

MI5   Military Intelligence, Section 5, is the United Kingdom's domestic counter-intelligence and security agency and is part of its intelligence machinery alongside the Secret Intelligence Service (MI6).

MSF   Medicins Sans Frontieres

NATO   North Atlantic Treaty Organization

NIA	National Intelligence Agency
RAND	Research and Development
RAW	Research and Analysis Wing
SAWW	'Sallalaahu alayhe wa alihi wa sallam', literally means may the Blessings of Allah be upon him (Prophet Muhammad) and his family (or his followers); and peace.
SBP	State Bank of Pakistan
RAA	'Razi Allah Anho', meaning May Allah be pleased with him. This term is used by Muslims with the names of the companions of the Prophet Muhammad.
RSS	Rashtriya Swayamsewak Sangh
SSG	Special Services Group
TTP	Tehrik-i-Taliban Pakistan
s.w.t	Subhanahu wa-ta'ala. It is an Arabic phrase that can be translated in English as: 'glorified and exalted be He' or 'may He be glorified and exalted' or 'he is glorified and exalted'.
UK	United Kingdom
UNO	United Nations Organization
US	United States
USA	United States of America
7/7	Terrorist attacks of 7th July, 2005 in London, UK
9/11	Terrorist attacks of 9th September, 2001 in USA

Chapter 1

TERRORISM – A GLOBAL MENACE

> *"Terrorism has no nationality or religion."*
>
> (**Vladimir Putin**, *Russian Statesman*) [1]

On September 11, 2001, at 8:45 a.m., an American Airlines Boeing 767 loaded with 20,000 gallons of fuel crashed into the north tower of the World Trade Center in the city of New York. I still vividly remember the day when I saw the horrific images of the 9/11 terrorist attacks on television upon returning from my office. Almost every news channel was covering the events of 9/11 in which nearly 3,000 innocent people were killed. According to telecasted news, 19 militants associated with an Islamic extremist group hijacked four airplanes and carried out the suicide attacks. Two planes were flown into the twin towers of the World Trade Center in New York, the third plane hit the Pentagon just outside Washington, D.C., and the fourth plane crashed in Pennsylvania.

The 9/11 attack on the World Trade Centre provided a set of powerful and dramatic images that, as a result of modern telecommunications, were rapidly transmitted around the globe. The images of the immediate aftermath were exhaustively replayed, analysed and pored over by horrified media audiences. Perhaps the shocking visual spectacle of the attack made it amenable to constant replay and expert analysis. Thus, as well as being a tragic act of terrorism, we can say that 9/11 also became a shared media experience.

The world changed drastically following the events of September 11, 2001. The world witnessed the aftereffects of the 9/11 terrorist attacks in which a major war against terrorism was launched by the United States and its allies. The US president at the time, President Bush, declared the 9/11 attacks an 'act of war' in an address to the Congress on September 20, 2001.

Bush's fervent speech, delivered very soon after the event, reflected the global revulsion sparked by the attack. For President Bush this meant the US and its allies had to embark on a 'war on terror' in response.

Since then, there is an ongoing war against terrorists all over the globe in which countries like Afghanistan and Iraq were invaded. Countless people were killed or affected in Iraq, Afghanistan, and other parts of the world in the process of this war on terror. The world also saw appalling images of severe human rights violations against detainees in the Abu Ghraib prison in Iraq after Iraq's invasion. The Abu Ghraib prison incidents received widespread condemnation both from within the United States and from abroad.

Many other nations, including some Muslim countries, are concurrently fighting their own war against terrorism because of the continued threat of terrorist attacks in their countries. Despite these concerted efforts at a global scale, spanning more than a decade, the menace of terrorism is still very much pervasive.

Many vicious terrorist attacks have taken place since 9/11 in different parts of the world. Some of the well-known attacks in Europe include the 2004 Madrid train bombings in Spain, the 2012 Toulouse and Montauban shootings in France and the 2005 London bombings in the United Kingdom, commonly known as the 7/7 London bombings. In the 7/7 London terrorist attack, four suicide bombers with rucksacks full of explosives attacked central London, killing 52 people and injuring hundreds more. It was the single worst terrorist atrocity on British soil.

Muslim countries have also faced the problem of terrorism with numerous attacks taking place in countries including Turkey, Saudi Arabia, Indonesia, Pakistan, Egypt, Bangladesh, and Yemen.

If we consider the case of Pakistan, the country has played one of the most active roles in the war against terrorism. Pakistan was even granted the status of a US non-NATO ally by the US government. Nevertheless, Pakistan is from among those countries that have suffered immensely during the war against terrorism. The magnitude of its losses can be gauged through the following 2017 report from a local newspaper:

"Terrorism during past decade and a half has taken a huge toll on Pakistan as more than 63,000 people lost their lives so far. Terrorism in Pakistan has become a major phenomenon from the past decade, relatively declining during recent few years. 62,096 are the number of fatalities from terrorist attacks from 2003 to 2017"

"…. Besides this, Pakistan's 'war on terror' has cost $118 billion so far, a report by the State Bank revealed in Nov 2016. The State Bank of Pakistan (SBP) in its annual report showed that extremist violence cost the country $118.3bn in direct and indirect losses from 2002 to 2016. Both economic growth and social sector development have been severely hampered by terrorism-related incidents,' the report said….Curiously, $118.3 billion, which Pakistan spent on 'war on terror', were enough to pay the total loan of Pakistan, if they were not spent to rid of the menace of terror from country in past 15 years." [2]

Since September 11, 2001, the world's attention has largely been focused on the violence of Islamic terrorism. This has also had negative repercussions for many Muslims, particularly those living in the West. The continuation of terrorist activities since 9/11, and the selective use of the terms 'terrorism' and 'terrorist attacks' by Western media and Western politicians reserved for Muslim terrorists, have created an atmosphere of Islamophobia in the Western world. As a result, the Muslim community at large, and especially those seen as more practicing, came under heavy suspicion in the West. Books like Londonistan [3] were published in the UK discussing the threat of Islam to Western society due to the rising number of Muslims in the UK.

An American Muslim writer Shawna Ayoub Ainslie who shared her post-9/11 experiences in a Huffington Post article, '20 Ways 9/11 Changed My Life as an (American) Muslim', writes:

"I was afraid to go outside. If I stayed inside, I couldn't mess up, except maybe with my words, which I policed carefully. I couldn't speed, I couldn't frighten anyone, I couldn't break any law — no matter how tenuous — and therefore couldn't be thrown in Gitmo." [4]

As part of the 9/11 aftermath, an abundance of scholarly work has been published by Western scholars in which they have tried to pinpoint the root causes of extremism and terrorism. Many people have tried to find the roots of terrorism in the religion of Islam by quoting various Islamic sacred texts out of context including verses of the Holy Quran, whereas some have made statements like "Not all Muslims are terrorists, but all terrorists are Muslims." Such false assertions and statements have been very upsetting to the majority of peace-loving Muslims.

Some have mixed or even equated the Islamic concept of Jihad with the current wave of global terrorism, while many have blamed the rise of so called 'Political Islam' as the root cause of terrorism.

It is true that being a complete religion, Islam has provided guidance regarding politics and war, but this does not at all mean that Islam teaches or encourages the killing of innocent people belonging to other religions, casts, or creeds.

Countless mainstream Islamic scholars have openly and emphatically denounced the acts of terrorism that have been carried out by a small number of Muslims. It is just as important to remember that Muslims have also been repeatedly targeted by terrorists in Muslim majority countries.

A USA Today article, 'Islamic State made Ramadan 2016 the bloodiest ever', reported:

"This year's month of daytime fasting and prayer (Muslim holy month of Ramadan) included a massive suicide bombing in Baghdad that killed nearly 300 people, an Istanbul airport attack that killed 45, a hostage-taking in Bangladesh that killed 22, an attack on security officials in Saudi Arabia, a bombing in Afghanistan that killed 64 and a shooting massacre at a gay nightclub in Orlando that killed 49. Most of the victims overseas were Muslim." [5]

In response, many prominent, unprejudiced non-Muslims have comprehended the suffering of Muslims at the hand of terrorists. For example, the Canadian prime minister Justin Trudeau tweeted after the 2016 terrorist incident in Iraq, "So-called Islamic State has again proven itself an enemy of all Muslims. My thoughts are with victims of the Ramadan attacks in Iraq". The attack which the Canadian prime minister is referring to resulted in the death of 300 people in Iraq. The attack was carried out during the Muslim holy month of Ramadan in which Muslims fast during the day and strive to engage in other religious and charitable activities.

The fallacy of the statement "Not all Muslims are terrorists, but all terrorists are Muslims" can be appreciated through the following words of the British historian Tony Judt:

"Even if we exclude assassinations or attempted assassinations of presidents and monarchs and confine ourselves to men and women who kill random unarmed civilians in pursuit of a political objective, terrorists have been with us for well over a century. There have been anarchist terrorists, Russian terrorists, Indian terrorists, Arab terrorists, Basque terrorists, Malay terrorists, Tamil terrorists, and dozens of others besides. There have been and still are Christian terrorists, Jewish terrorists, and Muslim terrorists. There were Yugoslav ("partisan") terrorists settling scores in World War II; Zionist terrorists blowing up Arab marketplaces in Palestine before 1948; American-financed Irish terrorists in Margaret Thatcher's London; US-armed mujahideen terrorists in 1980s Afghanistan; and so on." [7]

These quoted statements clearly support the counter-argument that terrorism has no nationality or religion.

I must also mention here that like in many other matters, numerous conspiracy theories have evolved around the 9/11 terrorist attacks and the ensuing war against terrorism. There are many such theories circulating in the world about events like the invasion of Iraq and the creation of ISIS (or ISIL). Occasionally, short video clips based on such conspiracy theories make their rounds on social media. Some Western writers have even written books dedicated to this subject. [8] However, even if these conspiracy theories are true, one cannot completely deny the fact that there have been some misguided Muslims who, in the past two decades, have been associated with either the planning or execution of terrorist attacks in various parts of the world.

The subsequent chapters of this book expand upon these matters along with other related topics. Chapter 2 covers the topic of extremism and terrorism in detail to provide a general, overarching understanding to readers. Chapter 3 gives the Islamic perspective on terrorism, explaining how such acts of violence are against the teachings of Islam. Chapter 4 discusses the political aspects of global extremism and terrorism. Chapter 5 discusses the topic of extremism and compares it with the teachings of Islam. Chapter 6 discusses the Islamic teachings regarding the treatment of non-Muslims. Chapter 7 elucidate the Islamic concept of Jihad and the teachings of Islam regarding the behavior of Muslim soldiers in the times of war.

Chapter 2

UNDERSTANDING EXTREMISM AND TERRORISM

"Everybody's worried about stopping terrorism. Well, there's a really easy way: stop participating in it."

(Noam Chomsky, *US intellectual & political activist)* [1]

Phrases like 'terrorism', 'terrorist', 'terrorist attacks', 'extremism', 'fundamentalism', and 'Jihad' gained visibility in the public eye after the 9/11 attacks in the USA. 'Terrorism', being the most popular among these, has become a commonly vocalized term, resorted to selectively by the global media while reporting certain acts of violence. It is necessary for us to understand the precise connotation of these terms to accurately comprehend the problem of terrorism and extremism in the world. This chapter provides a comprehensive analysis of the terms 'terrorism' and 'extremism', while chapter 6 analyses the Islamic concept of 'Jihad'.

DEFINING TERRORISM AND EXTREMISM

Defining certain concepts can be a difficult matter, especially when it comes to sensitive, complex issues like terrorism and extremism. There are several definitions of terrorism which sometimes paradoxically even seem mutually incompatible. These have also been contested by expressions like 'One man's terrorist is another man's freedom fighter'. Thus, there is no universal consensus when it comes to defining terrorism. Some adhere to a broad definition in which formal nation states can themselves be guilty of terrorism, while others strongly discard this view, describing terrorism instead as 'the use of violence against civilians by non-state actors'.

Some adhere to a broad definition of terrorism in which formal nation states can themselves be guilty of terrorism, while others strongly discard this view, describing terrorism instead as 'the use of violence against civilians by non-state actors'.

According to the Merriam-Webster dictionary, the term terrorism "came to English as translations of words used in French during the period known as the Reign of Terror (1793-94), when the new government punished—usually by death—those people thought to be against the ongoing French Revolution. It was a gruesome and protracted period of official state-sponsored violence that set the political tone for much of the use of these words ever since." [2]

With the passage of time, the connotation of many terms transforms, often widening to include other concepts and this has also been the case with the term 'terrorism'. The following are a selection of contemporary definitions of 'terrorism' as suggested by well-known dictionaries, encyclopedias, and organizations:

Oxford English Dictionary:

'The unlawful use of violence and intimidation, especially against civilians, in the pursuit of political aims.' [3]

Merriam Webster Dictionary:

'The systematic use of terror especially as a means of coercion.' [4]

Encyclopedia Brittanica:

'The systematic use of violence to create a general climate of fear in a population and thereby to bring about a particular political objective. Terrorism has been practiced by political organizations with both rightist and leftist objectives, by nationalistic and religious groups, by revolutionaries, and even by state institutions such as armies, intelligence services, and police.' [5]

Wikipedia:

'Terrorism is, in the broadest sense, the use of intentionally indiscriminate violence as a means to create terror, or fear, to achieve a political, religious or ideological aim."

"It is used in this regard primarily to refer to violence against peacetime targets or in war against non-combatants.' [6]

The United Nations:

In November 2004, a Secretary General of the United Nations report described terrorism as any act 'intended to cause death or serious bodily harm to civilians or non-combatants with the purpose of intimidating a population or compelling a government or an international organization to do or abstain from doing any act'.

In 2005, the United Nations (UN) proposed to define terrorism as something that involved 'any act intended to intimidate a population or to compel a government or an international body to act' and constituted 'one of the most serious threats to international peace and security'. However, in 2006, the 192 nation states comprising the UN failed to agree upon a formal definition. This was largely because of disagreements among members on whether a definition should encompass armed conflicts that take place in 'situations of foreign occupation'. [7]

US Federal Bureau of Investigation (FBI):

According to the FBI, 'There is no single, universally accepted, definition of terrorism. Terrorism is defined in the Code of Federal Regulations as 'the unlawful use of force and violence against persons or property to intimidate or coerce a government, the civilian population, or any segment thereof, in furtherance of political or social objectives". [8]

The quoted definitions above, though containing slight differences, consistently point towards the same general phenomenon.

We can extract the following key words from these definitions:

The use of violence against:

- Civilians

- Property

- Non-combatants during war

- Peacetime targets

Violence used by:

- (Unspecified)

Characteristics of violence:

- Intentional
- Indiscriminate
- Unlawful
- Systematic
- Intimidating

For coercing:

- The Government
- The civilian population
- Any segment of society
- Any international body

Result of violence:

- Intimidation
- Terror or fear

Aims:

- Political
- Religious
- Ideological

- Social

Although there is no single universally accepted definition of terrorism, if we try to wisely derive a comprehensive definition based on these extracted words, this definition would look something like:

'An intentional and unlawful use of violence or intimidation, whether by a state or a non-state actor, against civilians, property, peacetime targets, or non-combatants during war, that results in terror in order to coerce a government, civilian population, certain segment of society, or any international body to achieve one's political, religious, ideological, or social objectives.'

I will tend to follow this broader definition of terrorism in subsequent discussions of this book.

Another term that has received significant public attention in the post 9/11 world is the term 'extremism'. Terrorists themselves are sometimes referred to as extremists. In customary usage, the term 'extremism' is most often used in religious or political sense to refer to an ideology that is considered, either by the speaker or by some implied shared social consensus, to be far outside the acceptable mainstream attitudes or norms of society. However, extremism can also be used in an economic sense. Extremists are usually contrasted with moderates.

Some acclaimed sources have defined 'extremism' as:

Oxford English Dictionary:

'The holding of extreme political or religious views; fanaticism.' [9]

Merriam Webster Dictionary:

'The quality or state of being extreme.' [10]

Wikipedia:

'Extremism means, literally, the quality or state of being extreme or the advocacy of extreme measures or views.' [11]

TERRORIST INCIDENTS

From the bombing of public places to the hijacking of planes, terrorists have used an extensive range of methods and approaches to execute their plans. Innovative concepts like cyber-terrorism are also being employed now, causing the disruption or destruction of computers and networks of important organizations in a country. The most commonly known types of terrorist attacks include the following:

1. Bombings

2. Armed attacks and assassinations

3. Arson and fire bombings

4. Hijacking and skyjackings

5. Nuclear / Radiological / Biological / Chemical attacks

6. Kidnapping and hostage taking

7. Cyber-terrorism

However, other types of violence can also be perpetrated under the framework of terrorism. For example, terrorist groups may conduct maiming of their own people as a form of punishment for security violations, defections, or informants. Terrorist organizations may also be involved in robberies and extortion to finance their terrorist activities.

With the passage of time, some of these other forms of terrorism are also formally being recognized such as 'economic terrorism or financial terrorism' which is strictly defined to indicate an attempt for economic destabilization by a group'.

A more detailed description being "Contrary to 'economic warfare' which is undertaken by states against other states, economic terrorism is undertaken by transnational or non-state actors who could entail varied, coordinated and sophisticated or massive destabilizing actions in order to disrupt the economic and financial stability of a state, a group of states or a society or a trading exchange for ideological, monetary or religious motives."

MOTIVATIONS AND GOALS OF TERRORISTS

According to 'Terrorism-Research' website [12], terrorist groups commit acts of violence to:

- Produce widespread fear

- Obtain worldwide, national, or local recognition for their cause by attracting the attention of the media

- Harass, weaken, or embarrass government security forces so that the government overreacts and appears repressive

- Steal or extort money and equipment, especially weapons and ammunition vital to the operation of their group

- Destroy facilities or disrupt lines of communication in order to create doubt that the government can provide for and protect its citizens

- Discourage foreign investments, tourism, or assistance programs that can affect the target country's economy and support of the government in power

- Influence government decisions, legislation, or other critical decisions

- Free prisoners

- Satisfy vengeance

- Turn the tide in a guerrilla war by forcing government security forces to concentrate their efforts in urban areas. This allows the terrorist group to establish itself among the local populace in rural areas

Different terrorist ideologies are driven by their own set of beliefs that justify their violent behavior. In this way, to them, it is seen as serving a meaningful cause.

An examination of the history of terrorist incidents shows that terrorists can have secular as well as religious ideologies serving as their source of motivation.

They may even be funded by enemy states to carry out their operations in other countries. Moreover, terrorism can be inflicted by non-state or sub-state actors or even by the states itself in local or foreign lands.

The following sections of this chapter provide examples elaborating the various categories of extremism and terrorism.

RELIGIOUS EXTREMISM AND TERRORISM

On July 17, 2005, the London bombings resulted in 56 deaths and 784 injuries; on November 13, 2015, the Paris terrorist attacks resulted in 137 deaths and 413 injuries; on December 16, 2014, the Army Public School massacre in Pakistan resulted in 148 deaths and 114 injuries, and there have been similar attacks on shrines in Iraq and Syria. These are all examples of terrorist attacks carried out by people who professed Islamic motivations or goals, in which both Muslims and non-Muslims were targeted.

Since the 9/11 attacks in the USA, public attention has primarily been focused on acts of terrorism committed by Muslim fanatics. However, this does not mean that Muslims are exclusive perpetrators of terrorist activities in the world. The following discussion contains examples of extremists from other religions who have been responsible for the death and suffering of many innocent people in the name of religion.

Hindu extremism is on the rise in India. The article 'Christians and Muslims Face More Persecution by Hindu Extremists in India' mentions;

"Violent attacks on religious minorities in India averaged one attack per day last year, a rising number that has led a coalition of US Congress members to plead with India's leaders to condemn the violence. According to the Catholic Secular Forum, attacks rose more than 20 percent from 2014 to 2015. There have been 36 attacks on Christians so far this year, ranging from churches being destroyed to priests, nuns, and parishioners being beaten, according to the Christian human rights group International Christian Concern (ICC), as well as four murders of Muslim men by Hindu mobs over their consumption of beef.

Christian rights groups monitoring the violence say the attacks have coincided with a strong rise in Hindu nationalism, which encompasses a broad spectrum of Indian political movements, but centers around the idea that Hindu traditions and beliefs should serve as a guide for the state and its citizens."

"The more extreme Hindu nationalists are accused of mounting the attacks." [13]

The 2007 Samjhauta Express railway bombing in India was a terrorist attack that occurred on February 18, 2007, on the Samjhauta Express, a twice-weekly train service connecting Dehli, India, and Lahore, Pakistan. Of the 68 fatalities, the majority were Pakistani civilians, though the victims also included some Indians and three railway policemen. Later in 2012, Kamal Chauhan, a disgruntled worker of the Hindu revivalist Rashtriya Swayamsewak Sangh (RSS, National Volunteer Corp), was arrested by the National Intelligence Agency (NIA) of India in connection with the bombing. According to the NIA, Mr. Chauhan had planted the bombs on board the Samjhauta Express after undergoing training in arms and explosives in Haryana and Madhya Pradesh in India.

Christian extremists have employed terror tactics as well. For example, the Christian terrorist organization 'Army of God (AOG)' has been involved in the use of anti-abortion violence in the USA. According to the US Department of Justice and Department of Homeland Security's joint Terrorism Knowledge Base, the Army of God was formed in 1982 and is an underground terrorist organization active in the United States. In addition to numerous property crimes, the Army of God has committed acts of kidnapping, attempted murder, and murder. While sharing a common ideology and tactics, AOG members claim to rarely communicate. The organization forbids those who wish to "take action against baby killing abortionists" from discussing their plans with anyone in advance.

In another incident, on July 27, 2008, a Christian Right sympathizer, Jim David Adkisson, walked into the Tennessee Valley Unitarian Universalist Church in Knoxville, Tennessee during a children's play and began shooting people at random. As a result, two people were killed, while seven others were injured. Adkisson said he was motivated by a hatred of liberals. [14]

Similarly, after witnessing the escalation of Buddhist extremism, TIME magazine published an article, 'Straying From the Middle Way: Extremist Buddhist Monks Target Religious Minorities', chronicling this phenomenon in 2013. According to the article;

"In the reckoning of religious extremism — Hindu nationalists, Muslim militants, fundamentalist Christians, ultra-Orthodox Jews — Buddhism has largely escaped trial. To much of the world, it is synonymous with nonviolence and loving kindness, concepts propagated by Siddhartha Gautama, the Buddha, 2500 years ago. But like adherents of any religion, Buddhists and their holy men are not immune to politics and, on occasion, the lure of sectarian chauvinism."

The article also mentions;

"The fault lines of conflict are often spiritual, one religion chafing against another and kindling bloodletting contrary to the values girding each faith. Over the past year in parts of Asia, it is friction between Buddhism and Islam that has killed hundreds, mostly Muslims. The violence is being fanned by extremist Buddhist monks, who preach a dangerous form of religious chauvinism to their followers." [15]

The year 2017 has probably been the bloodiest with respect to the incidence of Buddhist extremism. While reporting the assaults in Myanmar inflicted by Buddhists on the Muslim minority in 2017, the newspaper Independent mentioned;

"International aid group Doctors Without Borders said its field survey has found at least 6,700 Rohingya Muslims were killed between August and September in a crackdown by Burma's security forces. The group, known by the acronym from its French name, MSF, said in a statement made available Thursday that it had conducted the survey in refugee camps in Bangladesh, and estimated that at least 6,700 Rohingya died in Burma's Rakhine state between 25 August and 24 September. About 630,000 Rohingya have fled Burma into Bangladesh to escape what the United Nations has called 'ethnic cleansing'

…According to MSF, the dead included at least 730 children younger than five. …MSF said that among children below the age of five, more than 59 per cent who were killed during that period were reportedly shot, 15 per cent burnt to death in their homes, 7 per cent beaten to death and 2 per cent died due to land mine blasts."

"... MSF said the numbers of deaths are likely to be an underestimation 'as we have not surveyed all refugee resettlements in Bangladesh because the surveys don't account for the families who never made it out of Burma'." [16]

These were some examples of extremism and terrorism where the perpetrators seemed to have been motivated by religious ideologies.

However, this is not the case in every incident of terrorism as evident from the following discussion.

SECULAR EXTREMISM AND TERRORISM

Most definitions of terrorism speak of 'political' objectives of terrorism. Many terrorists who themselves claim or are generally assumed to be religiously motivated, will have desired political objectives that they hope to achieve through their acts of terror. Some writers have even suggested that terrorism is the product of 'politics'. For example, in his article 'It's not the religion that creates terrorists, it's the politics', Mr. Giles Fraser mentions, "The radicalisation hypothesis steers us away from the real causes of terrorism – and enables the west to maintain its denial about a role in helping create it."[17]

The proceeding paragraphs contain examples of extremism and terrorism that had clear secular motives.

On April 19, 1995, the Oklahoma City bombing was carried out on Alfred P Murrah Federal Building in downtown Oklahoma City, Oklahoma, United States by Timothy McVeigh and Terry Nichols. The Oklahoma bombing killed 168 people, injured more than 680, and destroyed one-third of the building. The bomb blast destroyed or damaged 324 nearby buildings within a 16-block radius, shattered glass in 258 buildings, and destroyed 86 cars, causing an estimated damage of $652 million.

The Oklahoma City bombing was the deadliest terrorist attack on American soil until the 9/11 attacks. The chief perpetrators, Timothy McVeigh and Terry Nichols, met in 1988 at Fort Benning during basic training for the U.S. Army.

They expressed anger at the federal government's handling of the 1992 Federal Bureau of Investigation (FBI) standoff with Randy Weaver at Ruby Ridge as well as the Waco siege.

The famous anthrax attacks in the USA, which resulted in 5 fatalities and 17 injuries, is another such example.

From September 18 to October 9, 2001, a series of letters were mailed by an unknown source to several media news outlets and two United States' senators, containing the toxic chemical agent Anthrax in powdered form. The letters included notes that pointed to extremist religious groups. As several people were killed from Anthrax exposure, the level of anxiety in the US heightened. However, investigators soon became convinced that the attacks were not carried out by any foreign extremist religious group. Instead, the investigation began to focus on Dr. Bruce E. Ivins, a scientist employed at a Federal bio-defense laboratory, who soon became the FBI's primary suspect.

Dr. Ivins committed suicide on July 27, 2008. Several weeks later, US federal prosecutors announced that Dr. Ivins was the sole perpetrator of the Anthrax attacks, though the conclusion has been contested by some.

A third example is of the Basque separatist movement. For nearly a 1000 years the Basque people have inhabited the foothills of the Pyrenees Mountains around the Bay of Biscay in southern France and northern Spain. They are the oldest surviving ethnic group in Europe. The Basques' distinctive language and culture were periodically suppressed, giving rise to a modern, violent separatist movement. In 1959, a group of Basque nationalists founded ETA, or Euskadi Ta Askatasuna, Basque Homeland and Liberty. This is a separatist, socialist organization that has conducted numerous terrorist activities to try to break free from Spanish and French rule and establish an independent country. As a result of these terrorist activities, more than 800 people, including police officers, government leaders, and innocent civilians, have been killed through a combination of assassinations and bombings, while thousands have been injured, kidnapped, or robbed.

I think these three well-known examples are enough to prove my point that religiously motivated fanatics are not singularly responsible for all terrorist activities.

Even players and states proclaiming to be secular have been involved in terrorist activities within their state boundaries or in other states.

NON-STATE OR SUB-STATE ACTORS

Earlier discussions on terrorism in this chapter make it clear that there is a growing presence of non-state actors who hinge on the use of violence against nation states to accomplish their goals. Groups like Al-Qaeda, Tehrik-i-Taliban-Pakistan, and ISIS are all examples of such non-state actors who engage in violence in support of their objectives.

Contemporary international politics is based on the notion of nation-state sovereignty, which comprises of two broad principles:

1. Territoriality, where the state has a monopoly on the use of organized violence.

2. Non-interventionism, where states do not interfere in the internal affairs of other states unless they are themselves threatened by that state.

Both these doctrines are challenged in the world today by non-state actors. War-making is no longer the monopoly of nation states because a new type of warfare has emerged known as 'asymmetrical warfare'. This war is fought between states and non-state or sub-state actors who employ terrorism to advance their cause. In his book 'Predators and Parasites: Persistent Agents of Transnational Harm and Great Power Authority', Mr. Lowenheim explains:

"Since the late nineteenth century, only sovereign states have been acknowledged by international law to possess the legal and customary right to employ transborder violence. In fact, war came to be characterized as a 'right inherent in sovereignty itself.' Moreover, the war making right was thought of as the paramount attribute to sovereignty."

"Today, only a sovereign state has the privilege to issue a transborder armed challenge to another state. Thus, international war also became a practice of exclusion and a device to set a group (of states) apart from other wielders of force. Historically, however, sovereignty and actorhood in the sphere of transborder violence were not identical. Between the sixteenth and mid nineteenth centuries, nonstate extraterritorial wielders of violence—such as mercenaries, brigands, filibusters, pirates, and privateers—often practiced transborder violence either independently or in the official service of sovereign states."

"In addition, nonsovereign polities claimed the legitimate right to order and authorize transborder violence. However, as Thomson and Spruyt have shown, states gradually delegitimized nonstate and nonsovereign violence and its wielders and avoided using it as a resource—initially because it was seen as a counterproductive and later because it was considered immoral as well.

States constructed a cartel of sovereigns that prohibited other actors from ordering and employing intensive transborder violence. In effect, sovereign states today constitute an elite club in world politics that excludes nonsovereign and nonstate authorizers and wielders of transborder force. The 9/11 attacks alerted the members of this club to the efforts of outsiders to change the rules for admission. Part of the trauma of 9/11 was precisely related to the realization that this elite club of states had been invaded by predatory nonstate actors thought to have disappeared two hundred years ago." [18]

STATE SPONSORSHIP

As mentioned previously, when defining terrorism some will absolve states from any association with terrorism, describing terrorism strictly as 'the use of violence against civilians by non-state actors to attain political goals', while others offer more broadened definitions to allow for state perpetration or connivance. I tend to support the latter view, otherwise one would have to negate various forms of existing terrorism involving nation states including so call 'rogue states'.

There are instances when governments themselves commit or support terrorist acts, utilizing terror to accomplish their objectives or the objectives of their rulers. Internal security forces may use terror to aid in repressing dissent, and intelligence or military organizations may execute acts of terror designed to further a country's policy or diplomatic efforts abroad. According to the 'Terrorism-Research' website [19]:

"Three different ways that states can engage in the use of terror are:

1. Governmental or 'State' terror

2. State involvement in terror

3. State sponsorship of terrorism and extremism"

"Governmental or State terror:

Sometimes referred to as 'terror from above', where a government terrorizes its own population to control or repress them. These actions usually constitute the acknowledged policy of the government, and make use of official institutions such as the judiciary, police, military, and other government agencies. Changes to legal codes permit or encourage torture, killing, or property destruction in pursuit of government policy. After assuming power, official Nazi policy was aimed at the deliberate destruction of 'state enemies' and the resulting intimidation of the rest of the population. Stalin's 'purges' of the 1930s are examples of using the machinery of the state to terrorize a population. The methods he used included such actions as rigged show trials of opponents, punishing family or friends of suspected enemies of the regime, and extra-legal use of police or military force against the population."

"State involvement in terror:

These are activities where government personnel carry out operations using terror tactics. These activities may be directed against other nations' interests, its own population, or private groups or individuals viewed as dangerous to the state. In many cases, these activities are terrorism under official sanction, although such authorization is rarely acknowledged openly.

Another type of these activities is 'death squads' or 'war veterans': unofficial actions taken by officials or functionaries of a regime (such as members of police or intelligence organizations) against their own population to repress or intimidate. While these officials will not claim such activities, and disguise their participation, it is often made clear that they are acting for the state. Keeping such activities "unofficial" permits the authorities deniability and avoids the necessity of changing legal and judicial processes to justify oppression. This is different than "pro-state" terror, which is conducted by groups or persons with no official standing and without official encouragement."

"While pro-state terror may result in positive outcomes for the authorities, their employment of criminal methods and lack of official standing can result in disavowal and punishment of the terrorists, depending on the morality of the regime in question."

"State sponsorship of terrorism:

Also known as 'state supported' terrorism, when governments provide supplies, training, and other forms of support to non-state terrorist organizations. One of the most valuable types of this support is the provision of safe haven or physical basing for the terrorists' organization. Another crucial service a state sponsor can provide is false documentation, not only for personal identification (passports, internal identification documents), but also for financial transactions and weapons purchases. Other means of support are access to training facilities and expertise not readily available to groups without extensive resources. Finally, the extension of diplomatic protections and services, such as immunity from extradition, diplomatic passports, use of embassies and other protected grounds, and diplomatic pouches to transport weapons or explosives have been significant to some groups."

Countries will often accuse each other of sponsoring terrorism, while the country claiming to be targeted may itself be sponsoring terrorism on foreign soil. The British author Ben Dupre, in his book '50 Political Ideas you really need to know' explains:

"States are sometimes accused of 'sponsoring' terrorism, usually with the implication that they are involved in giving financial or other indirect support to those committing violent acts in other countries. There is often a whiff of hypocrisy in such charges, however as in the 1980s, when the Reagan administration in the US accused Libya of sponsoring terrorism while simultaneously supporting violence against constitutional governments in the Nicaragua and elsewhere." [20]

To consider one case, India has bemoaned terrorist incidents that have tragically occurred within its borders but evidence has surfaced of its involvement in sponsoring terrorism in neighboring countries.

The Tamil Tigers were supported by the Indian government and were eventually defeated by the Sir Lankan government after a nearly 27 year long civil war.

India also actively supports terrorism in Pakistan. Chuck Hagel, President Barack Obama's Defence Secretary, discussed this during his speech at Cameron University in Oklahoma city, USA:

"India for some time has always used Afghanistan as a second front, and India has over the years financed problems for Pakistan on that side of the border. And you can carry that into many dimensions, the point being (that) the tense, fragmented relationship between Pakistan and Afghanistan has been there for many, many years." [21]

According to a leaked US embassy cable in 2010, Pakistani Prime Minister Gilani told US Senator John Kerry that "India had to decrease its footprint in Afghanistan and stop interfering in Baluchistan" in order to achieve confidence. Pakistan has regularly been vocal about RAW, the Indian military intelligence agency, of sending intelligence personnel into Afghanistan in the pretext of engineers and doctors, and of providing armed support to a militant group, the Baluchistan Liberation Army (BLA), involved in conducting many attacks on Pakistani civilians and security personnel. [22]

India has actively funded Baloch militants, hailing from Pakistan's largest province in terms of land area, to conduct terrorist activities in Pakistan. The U.S. magazine Foreign Affairs (March 2009) published the report of a roundtable discussion on the causes of instability in Pakistan.

Christine Fair of RAND Corporation said, "having visited the Indian mission in Zahedan, Iran, I can assure you they are not issuing visas as the main activity. Indian officials have told me privately that they are pumping money into Balochistan." [23]

For a long time, Pakistani intelligence agencies have pointed towards an element of foreign hands in terrorist attacks taking place in Pakistan. Subsequently, an Indian spy, Kulbhushan Sudhir Jadhav (also spelled Kulbhushan Yadav, alias Hussain Mubarak Patel), was arrested in Balochistan, Pakistan on March 3, 2016, over charges of terrorism and spying for India's intelligence agency---Research and Analysis Wing (RAW).

In order to give the reader an idea of how some states are involved in supporting terrorist activities on foreign soil, I am reproducing Kulbhushan Jadhav's confessional statement below which was made after his arrest.

"My name is Commander Kulbhushan Yadav and I am the serving officer of Indian Navy. I am from the cadre of engineering department of Indian Navy and my cover name was Hussein Mubarik Patel, which I had taken for doing some intelligence gathering for Indian agencies.

I joined the National Defence Academy in 1987 and subsequently joined Indian Navy in Jan 1991 and subsequently served for the Indian Navy till around December 2001 when the Parliament attack occurred and that is when I started contributing my services towards gathering of information and intelligence within India.

I live in the city of Mumbai in India. I am still the serving officer in the Indian Navy and will be due for retirement by 2022 as a commissioned officer in Indian Navy after having completed 14 years of service by 2002.

I commenced intelligence operation in 2003 and established a small business in Chabahar in Iran as I was able to achieve undetected existence and visits to Karachi in 2003 and 2004 and having done some basic assignments within India for RAW.

I was picked up by RAW in 2013 end."

"Ever since I have been directing various activities in Balochistan and Karachi (in Pakistan) at the behest of RAW and deteriorating law and order situation in Karachi, I was basically the man for Mr. Anil Kumar Gupta who is the joint secretary of RAW and his contacts in Pakistan especially in Balochistan Student Organisation.

My purpose was to hold meetings with Baloch insurgents and carry out activities with their collaboration. These activities have been of criminal nature, leading to killing of or maiming of Pakistani citizens.

I realise during this process that RAW is involved in some activities related to the Baloch liberation movement within Pakistan and the region around it.

There are finances which are fed into the Baloch movement through various contacts or various ways and means into the Baloch liberation (movement) and various activities of the Baloch liberation and RAW handlers go towards activities which are criminal, which are anti-national, which can lead to maiming or killing of people within Pakistan and mostly these activities were centred around of what I have knowledge is of ports of Gwadar, Pasni Jewani and various other installations, which are around the coast damaging various other installations, which are in Balochistan.

So the activity seems to be revolving and trying to create a criminal sort of mindset within the Baloch liberation which leads to instability within Pakistan. In my pursuit towards achieving the set targets by my handlers in RAW, I was trying to cross over into Pakistan from the Saravan border in Iran on March 3, 2016, and was apprehended by Pakistani authorities while on the Pakistani side and the main aim of this crossing over into Pakistan was to hold (a) meeting with Baloch separatists in Balochistan for carrying out various activities, which they were supposed to undertake and carrying backwards the messages which had to deliver to Indian agencies.

The main issues regarding this were that they were planning to conduct some operations within the next immediate (near) future so that was to be discussed mainly and that was the main aim of trying to coming into Pakistan."

"So that moment I realised that my intelligence operations have been compromised on my being detained in Pakistan, I revealed that I am an Indian naval officer, and it is on mentioning that I am Indian naval officer, the total perception of the establishment of the Pakistani side changed and they treated me very honourably and they did utmost respect and due regards and have handled me subsequently on a more professional and proper courteous way and they have handled me in a way that befits that of an officer and once I realised that I have been compromised in my process of intelligence operations, I decided to just end the mess I have landed myself in and just wanted to subsequently move on and cooperate with the authorities in removing complications which I have landed myself and my family members into, and whatever I am stating just now, it is the truth and it is not under any duress or pressure. I am doing it totally out of my own desire to mention and come clean out of this entire process which I have gone through last 14 years." [24]

On April 10, 2017, Jadhav was sentenced to death by a Field General Court Martial (FGCM) in Pakistan. On May 18, 2017, the International Court of Justice stayed his hanging, after it was approached by India, in opposition of the death sentence. Kulbhushan Jadhav was allowed to meet his wife and mother on December 25, 2017, by the Pakistani government; a staff member of the Indian embassy was also allowed to be present during this meeting.

VICTIMS OF TERRORISM

Many terrorist attacks are wholly directed at civilian populations, resulting in immeasurable suffering and losses of the general public who have nothing to do with state policies. The 9/11 terrorist attacks in the USA and the 7/7 terrorist attacks in the UK are examples of such attacks.

Before the 20th century warfare drew a distinguishing line between war combatants and non-combatants. Due to this, combatants were the principal targets of enemies, although non-combatants were frequently endangered and civilian casualties were common. Modern asymmetric warfare disregards such non-combatant immunity.

Therefore, civilians have been increasingly placed on the front lines of modern asymmetric warfare. With fewer state-versus-state wars since 1945, states are facing more and more wars with non-state and sub-state actors. Mary Kaldor of London School of Economics explains:

".... In conventional or regular war, the goal is the capture of territory by military means; battles are the decisive encounters of the war. Guerrilla warfare developed as a means of getting around the massive concentrations of military force which are characteristics of conventional war. In guerrilla warfare, territory is captured through political control of the population rather than through military advance .... Hence the strategic goal of these wars is to mobilise extremist politics based on fear and hatred. This often involves population expulsion through various means such as mass killing and forcible resettlement, as well as a range of political, psychological and economic techniques of intimidation."

".... At the turn of the twentieth century, the ratio of military to civilian casualties in wars was 8:1. Today, this has been almost exactly reversed ... the ratio of military to civilian casualties is approximately 1: 8 ...." [25]

Most heartbreakingly, some terrorist attacks have even been so barbaric as to solely target innocent children. Today is the 16th of December; few years ago, on this very date, six terrorists attacked a children's school in Pakistan, and so I write today with a very heavy heart. What I am referring to is the December 16, 2014 terrorist attack by Tehrik-i-Taliban-Pakistan (TTP) at the Army Public School in Peshawer, Pakistan. 132 children were killed in this attack along with other staff members present in the school. A rescue operation was launched by the Pakistan Army's Special Services Group (SSG) special forces, who killed all six terrorists and rescued 960 people.

I am ending this chapter with the English translation of the Urdu poetry released by the Pakistan Army 'Inter Services Public Relations' (ISPR) as a tribute to the martyred children in this utterly horrifying attack.

What is he searching for, I live on in books
I will be found in the promises I made to my mother

I am the future, how can he slay me today?
He has to be delusional if he believes he can kill such dreams

I am your blood, hence I've fought valiantly
I have proven to the enemy that I am better than him

I am from the nation whose children frighten him
Some enemy he is, he who targets children

So when you hugged me as I departed
You did not wish me Aman'Allah (within God's safety)

How did he cross into God's path of peace?
He desecrated my forehead where you used to kiss me, mother

I am from the nation whose children frighten him
Some enemy he is, he who targets children

Although I have been forced to leave, my brother will take my place
He will continue the education that I have been deprived of

My father is alive, you won't find refuge anywhere
Be rest assured, you won't come here, ever again

I am from the nation whose children frighten him
Some enemy he is, he who targets children!

Chapter 3

ISLAM AND TERRORISM

"Words of Muslims are important. It's important for people to know that Muslims think that terrorism is the epitome of injustice because it targets innocent people. People need to hear those words, and they're more credible from Muslims themselves."

*(**Karen Hughes,** Former US Undersecretary of State for Public Diplomacy & Public Affairs)* [1]

Some readers of my books are non-Muslims who have no, or very little, knowledge about Islam. Moreover, the sole source of that 'little knowledge' is likely the mass media which relentlessly associates 'Islam' and 'Muslims' with terrorism. I therefore feel it is necessary to provide a brief introduction of Islam in this chapter before delving into further discussions. I also recommend Muslim readers to go through this brief introduction.

ISLAM – AN INTRODUCTION

In Arabic the word 'Islam' means "submission", meaning submission to the will of God. Islam also means "peace", the peace one finds through submission to the will of God. The term 'Deen of Islam' can be defined as a collection of all those matters of obedience that Allah (God Almighty), through His Messengers, has made obligatory upon people, by means of which His (God's) nearness and mercy are received.

The Deen of Islam consists of the following teachings:

1. Basic matters and concepts that do not change with time e.g. tenets of faith like belief in one God, the belief that God's commandments must be obeyed, and basic teachings of morality and ethics like speaking the truth. These concepts were conveyed to mankind, without any alteration, by every Prophet sent by God throughout human history.

2. However, there are other matters that changed with time depending upon the need of the time. For example, certain commandments that were given to Hazrat Musa AS (Moses) changed during the prophethood of Hazrat Esa AS (Jesus). In the Quran, Prophet Esa AS (Jesus) is reported to have said to the Children of Israel, "(I have come to you) to attest the Law which was before me and to make lawful to you part of what was (before) forbidden to you; I have come to you with a Sign from your Lord. So fear Allah and obey me." (Surah Al-i-Imran, Chapter 3, Ayat 50)

Present day adherents of the religion of Islam, called Muslims, believe Islam is the final message from God to mankind. It is a reconfirmation and perfection of the messages that God revealed through earlier Prophets. According to Islamic Fiqah (jurisprudence) literature, the Deen of Islam guides us in five types of matters:

1. DOGMAS (A system of belief): Belief in 'one God i.e Allah', 'Angels', 'Holy Books' like the Quran and Bible, 'Prophets', 'The Day of Judgment', to name a few.

2. ACTS OF WORSHIP: Salat (prayer), Zakat (charity), Saum (fasting), Hajj (pilgrimage), and Jihad (which means "to struggle or strive, to exert oneself" for a praiseworthy aim).

3. DEALINGS: Such as financial matters, family matters, conflict resolution and judicial matters, inheritance matters, and trust related matters.

4. PUNISHMENTS: For example, punishments for murder, expropriation of property, adultery/fornication, false allegation of adultery/fornication, and apostasy.

5. MANNERS: Ethics and morality, etiquettes and social virtues, government related matters, and other social matters [2].

In August 1941, the founder of Pakistan, Quaid-e-Azam Muhammad Ali Jinnah, went to Hyderabad Deccan (India) and gave an interview to the students of Usmania University. His reply to the question "What are the essential features of religion and a religious State?" was:

"When I hear the word 'religion,' my mind thinks at once, according to the English language and the British usage, of private relation between man and God. But I know fully well that according to Islam, the word is not restricted to the English connotation. I am neither a Maulvi nor a Mulla, nor do I claim knowledge of theology. But I have studied in my own way, the Holy Quran and Islamic tenets. This magnificent Book is full of guidance respecting all human life, whether spiritual or economic, political or social, leaving no aspect untouched." [3]

The world renowned Islamic scholar Mufti Muhammad Taqi Usmani further elaborates this concept:

"He (God) has created man and appointed him as His vicegerent on the earth to fulfill certain objectives through obeying His commands. These commands are not restricted to some modes of worship or so-called religious rituals. They, on the contrary, cover a substantial area of almost every activity of life. These commands are neither so exhaustive that straiten the human activities within a narrow circle, leaving no room for human intellect to play, nor they are so little and ambiguous that they leave every sphere of life at the mercy of human perception and desire. Far from these two extremes, Islam has a balanced approach to govern the human life. On the one hand, it has left a wide area of human activities to man's own rational judgment where he can take decisions on the basis of his reason, assessment of facts and expedience.

On the other hand, Islam has subjected human activities to a set of principles which have eternal application and cannot be violated on superficial grounds of expediency based on human assessment. The fact behind this scheme is that human reason, despite vast capabilities, cannot claim to have unlimited power to reach the truth. There are numerous domains of the human life where 'reason' is often confused with 'desires' and where unhealthy instincts, under the disguise of rational arguments misguide humanity to wrong and destructive decisions.

All those theories of the past which are held today to be fallacious, claimed, in their respective times, to be 'rational' but it were after centuries that their fallacy was discovered and their absurdity was universally proved. It is thus evident that the sphere of work delegated to human 'reason' by its Creator is not unlimited."

"There are areas in which human reason cannot give proper guidance or, at least, is susceptible to errors. It is these areas in which Allah Almighty, the Creator of the universe, has provided guidance through His revelations sent down to His Prophets." [4]

Sources of Islamic Law:

The two main sources for deriving Islamic law (also commonly referred to as Shariah law) are 1) The Holy Quran, and 2) The life and teachings of Prophet Muhammad (S.A.W.W). The interpretation and practice of Prophet Muhammad (S.A.W.W)'s Companions (also known as Sahaba) are given priority in understanding these two sources as they were present at the time the Quran was being revealed to mankind via His last messenger, Prophet Muhammad (S.A.W.W), and were trained directly by the Prophet (S.A.W.W) himself.

In deriving Islamic law, Muslim jurists also sometimes use the processes of 'Ijmaa' and 'Qiyaas'. 'Ijmaa' is the term used for an opinion or command of Islam where all good and respected scholars (upright, qualified, reliable and trustworthy scholars) of Islam are unanimous in their ruling. 'Qiyaas' is a process whereby a clear ruling of the permissibility or impermissibility of an act or matter is applied to an issue closest in relation to it.

Islamic scholars:

A formally trained scholar of Islam is called an 'Alim (plural Ulema)' who graduates in Islamic studies from a traditional Islamic school called a 'madrassa' (school) or 'Jamia' (university). After receiving a degree in Islamic studies, an Alim can further specialize to become a 'Mufti' who can issue a 'Fatwa' on various matters. A 'Fatwa' is an Islamic legal pronouncement issued by an expert in religious law, usually at the request of an individual or judge, to resolve an issue where Islamic jurisprudence (fiqh) is unclear.

Other than qualified Ulema and Muftis from traditional Islamic schools and universities, there are numerous Islamic scholars and intellectuals who have gained knowledge of Islam through their formal and/or informal study of Islam.

Readers who are interested in learning further about Islam can consult my book ISLAM: A SUPERIOR SYSTEM OF LIFE [5], which provides a comprehensive analysis of the religion and compares its teachings with other popular systems like Capitalism and Communism.

DOES ISLAM SUPPORTS TERRORISM?

A few days ago, after having decided to write this book, I went to visit a Mufti, Mufti Nazeer Ahmed, to explore his views on terrorism. He belongs to Jamia Binoria which is an international Islamic educational institute in Karachi, Pakistan. Mufti Nazeer Ahmed often appears on a local television channel in a religious morning program. I posed the hypothetical question to him that if someone sets a bomb in a public place of a Western, non-Muslim country that eventually takes numerous innocent lives, what would be his point of view regarding this violent act? While I was still in the process of putting the question to him, he began to stare me astonishingly as if to suggest how I could even raise such a question. I told him that I know the right answer, but I just wanted to know his point of view. He immediately replied that this would be a grossly iniquitous act, after which he gave me a more detailed explanation.

Based on his explanation, there are many instructions in the Quran for mankind; these can be classified into instructions for individuals and instructions for the state. For example, the instruction to fast during the holy month of Ramazan is for individuals, whereas the instructions related to punishing criminals in a certain prescribed manner are for the state. Therefore, an individual cannot administer punishments to criminals on his or her own. Similarly, Quranic instructions pertaining to matters like war, jihad, etc., are for the state. Thus, an individual or non-state actor cannot go to a foreign land in order to start an armed conflict.

Mufti Nazeer Ahmed had previously authored a paper on the topic 'Rules and Morality of Wars in Islam'. In his paper he writes, "One of the principles of war (in Islam) is that one should only fight with those who are able to fight. Those who cannot fight or do not wish to fight, shall not be killed."

Hence, non-combatants cannot be killed even in the context of wars. I have reproduced some portions of his paper in the final chapter of this book.

We derived the following broad definition of terrorism in Chapter 2 of this book:

'An intentional and unlawful use of violence or intimidation, whether by a state or a non-state actor, against civilians, property, peacetime targets, or non-combatants during war, that results in terror in order to coerce a government, civilian population, certain segment of society, or any international body to achieve one's political, religious, ideological, or social objectives.'

In view of the previously quoted discussion of Mufti Nazeer Ahmed alongside this definition of terrorism, the reader can conclusively discern that there is no place for terrorism in Islam. This is why the mainstream Muslim majority has always denounced terrorist attacks.

The following section contains statements made by various Muslim scholars in response to 9/11, 7/7, and other terrorist attacks in the Western world:

Statements/Fatwas by Muslim scholars: [6]

The following is a joint statement made by Mustafa Mashhur, General Guide, Muslim Brotherhood, Egypt; Qazi Hussain Ahmed, Ameer, Jamaat-e-Islami Pakistan, Pakistan; Muti Rahman Nizami, Ameer, Jamaat-e-Islami Bangladesh, Bangladesh; Shaykh Ahmad Yassin, Founder, Islamic Resistance Movement (Hamas), Palestine; Rashid Ghannoushi, President, Nahda Renaissance Movement, Tunisia; Fazil Nour, President, PAS – Parti Islam SeMalaysia, Malaysia; and 40 other Muslim scholars and politicians:

"The undersigned, leaders of Islamic movements, are horrified by the events of Tuesday 11 September 2001 in the United States which resulted in massive killing, destruction and attack on innocent lives. We express our deepest sympathies and sorrow. We condemn, in the strongest terms, the incidents, which are against all human and Islamic norms. This is grounded in the Noble Laws of Islam which forbid all forms of attacks on innocents. God Almighty says in the Holy Qur'an: 'No bearer of burdens can bear the burden of another' (Surah al-Isra 17:15)." [7]

Statement of Abdul Aziz bin Abdallah Al-Ashaykh, Chief Mufti of Saudi Arabia:

"Firstly: the recent developments in the United States including hijacking planes, terrorizing innocent people and shedding blood, constitute a form of injustice that cannot be tolerated by Islam, which views them as gross crimes and sinful acts. Secondly: any Muslim who is aware of the teachings of his religion and who adheres to the directives of the Holy Qur'an and the Sunnah (the teachings of the Prophet Muhammad) will never involve himself in such acts, because they will invoke the anger of God Almighty and lead to harm and corruption on earth." (Statement of September 15, 2001)

Council of Saudi 'Ulama, fatwa issued in February 2003:

"What is happening in some countries from the shedding of the innocent blood and the bombing of buildings and ships and the destruction of public and private installations is a criminal act against Islam. ... Those who carry out such acts have the deviant beliefs and misleading ideologies and are responsible for the crime. Islam and Muslims should not be held responsible for such actions." [8]

Harun Yahya (Adnan Oktar), Turkish author:

"The religion of Islam can by no means countenance terrorism. On the contrary, terror (i.e. murder of innocent people) in Islam is a great sin, and Muslims are responsible for preventing these acts and bringing peace and justice to the world." [9]

Mufti Nizamuddin Shamzai, Head Mufti at Jamiat-ul-Uloom-ul-Islamia seminary, Binori Town, Pakistan and a leader of the Jamiat Ulema-e-Islam (JUI) party, Pakistan:

"It's wrong to kill innocent people. ... It's also wrong to praise those who kill innocent people." [10]

Fatwa signed by more than 500 British Muslim scholars, clerics, and imams:

"Islam strictly, strongly and severely condemns the use of violence and the destruction of innocent lives. There is neither place nor justification in Islam for extremism, fanaticism or terrorism. Suicide bombings, which killed and injured innocent people in London, are HARAAM – vehemently prohibited in Islam, and those who committed these barbaric acts in London [on July 7, 2005] are criminals not martyrs. Such acts, as perpetrated in London, are crimes against all of humanity and contrary to the teachings of Islam. ... The Holy Quran declares: 'Whoever kills a human being... then it is as though he has killed all mankind; and whoever saves a human life, it is as though he had saved all mankind.' (Quran, Surah al-Maidah (5), verse 32) Islam's position is clear and unequivocal: Murder of one soul is the murder of the whole of humanity; he who shows no respect for human life is an enemy of humanity." [11]

Shaykh Abdul Aziz Al-Asheikh, Chief Mufti of Saudi Arabia on the London attacks:

"...targeting peaceful people, are not condoned by Islam, and are indeed prohibited by our religion. ... Attributing to Islam acts of individual or collective killings, bombings, destruction of properties and the terrorizing of peaceful people is unfair, because they are alien to the divine religion."(Fatwa-Online, July 9, 2005)

Maulana Marghubur Rahman, organizer of "Anti-Terrorism Convention" and rector of the Darul-Ulum Deoband madrasa, India:

"We condemn all forms of terrorism … and in this we make no distinction. Terrorism is completely wrong, no matter who engages in it, and no matter what religion he follows or community he belongs to." (February 2008)

Muhammad Tahir-ul-Qadri, founding leader of Minhaj-ul-Quran International, Pakistan:

"The killing of Muslims and the perpetration of terrorism are not only unlawful and forbidden in Islam but also represent the rejection of faith."

Muhammad Tahir-ul-Qadri has issued a 512 page detailed Fatwa against terrorism and suicide bombings.

According to the National Post of Canada: Syed Soharwardy, an imam at the Al-Madinah Calgary Islamic Centre, who organized the initiative, said that any attack by foreign elements should also be considered a direct affront to the 10 million Muslims who call either Canada or the United States home. "We want Muslims around the world who would dare to commit terrorism on our soil to know that we stand together with all Canadians and Americans." "We are asking Muslims here not only to condemn terrorism but to also see these events as attacks on themselves."

FATWA: "We, the undersigned Imams, are issuing the following Fatwa in order to guide the Muslims of North America regarding the attacks on Canada and the United States by the terrorists and the extremists,"

"In our view, these attacks are evil and Islam requires from Muslims to stand up against this evil. In the holy Qur'an Almighty Allah (God) orders Muslims:

"Let there among you be a group that summon to all that is beneficial commands what is proper and forbids what is improper; they are the ones who will prosper." (3:104)

"Believing men and believing women are protecting friends of one another; they enjoin what is right and forbid what is wrong; they perform salat and give zakat…" (9:71)

"Our beloved Prophet Muhammad (peace be upon him) said in a Hadith;

"When people see a wrong-doer and do nothing to stop him, they may well be visited by God with a punishment."

"Therefore, it is an obligation upon us (Imams) to inform all Muslims around the world that Muslims in Canada and the United States have complete freedom to practice Islam.

"There is no single city in Canada and the United States where MASAJIDS (Mosques) are not built. In all major cities Islamic schools provide education to Muslim children about Qur'an and the Islamic traditions.

"Thousands of Muslims perform Hajj every year and travel to Saudi Arabia with complete freedom and respect. In the month of Ramadan, both Canadian and the United States governments recognize the occasion and greet all Muslim citizens.

"Muslims pray five daily prayers in mosques without any fear or restrictions. Muslims have complete freedom to pay Zakat (poor due) to the charity or a person of their choice. Muslims have complete freedom to celebrate their festivals openly, publicly and Islamically. Muslims enjoy freedom of religion just like Christians, Jews and others. No one stops us from obeying Allah and His Messenger (Peace be upon him). No one stops us from preaching Islam and practicing Islam. In many cases, Muslims have more freedom to practice Islam here in Canada and the United States than many Muslim countries."

"In fact, the constitutions of the United States and Canada are very close to the Islamic guiding principles of human rights and freedom. There is no conflict between the Islamic values of freedom and justice and the Canadian /US values of freedom and justice."

"Therefore, any attack on Canada and the United States is an attack on the freedom of Canadian and American Muslims. Any attack on Canada and the United States is an attack on thousands of mosques across North America. It is a duty of every Canadian and American Muslim to safeguard Canada and the USA.

"They must expose any person, Muslim OR non-Muslim, who would cause harm to fellow Canadians OR Americans. We, Canadian and American Muslims, must condemn and stand up against these attacks on Canada and the United States. May Allah (God) save Canada, the United States and the entire world from the evil of wrong doers. Ameen."

Signed by: Prof. Imam Syed B. Soharwardy – Calgary, Allama Imam Ghalib Hussain Chishty – Calgary, Allama Imam Syed Mukhtar Naeemi – Houston, USA, Allama Imam Muhammad Nasir Qadri – Montreal, Allama Imam Abdul Latif No'mani – Vancouver, Imam Hafiz Muhammad Zarif Naeemi – Calgary, Imam Nizamuddin Sayed Qadri – Calgary, Imam Qazi Bashiruddin Qadri – Hamilton, Imam Osman Qazi – Toronto, Imam Saeed Ahmed Saifee – Toronto, Alimah Hafizah Sister Zaheera Tariq – Calgary, Imam Ayaz Khan Qadri –

Calgary, Alimah Sister Fatimah Zohra – Toronto, Imam Shahid Bashir Lahori – Calgary, Imam Hafiz Intizar Ahmed Qadri – Montreal, Imam Sayed Sajid Qadri – Calgary, Imam Arif Mahmood Naqshbandi – Calgary, Imam Muhammad Anees Siddiqui – Calgary, Sister Shahana Kamil – Mississauga, and Mr. Mushtaq Khan – Mississauga

In 2014, more than 120 Muslim leaders and scholars co-signed an open letter to Abu Bakr al-Baghdadi, the leader of ISIS, arguing that the establishment and practices of the Islamic State caliphate are not legitimate in Islam. The letter includes a technical point-by-point criticism of ISIS' actions and ideology based on the Quran and classical religious texts. This letter is not the first instance of ISIS being openly denounced by Islamic scholars. [12]

The aforementioned discussion and quoted statements of various Muslim scholars make it crystal clear that there is no place for terrorism in Islam. Islam does not, in any way, sanction or approve taking the lives of innocent people, whether they are Muslims or non-Muslims. In Ulema's (Islamic scholars) opinion, terrorism related crimes fall in the category of "hirabah" and those practicing it shall be punished according to the following verses of the Holy Qur'an:

"Those who fight against Allah and His Messenger and run about trying to spread disorder on the earth, their punishment is no other than that they shall be killed, or be crucified, or their hands and legs be cut off from different sides, or they be kept away from the land (they live in). That is a humiliation for them in this world, and for them there is a great punishment in the Hereafter." (Surah Al-Maida, Chapter 5, Ayat 33)

RELIGIOUS PIETY AND TERRORISM

Someone very aptly stated, "Don't always look at Muslims. Look at Islam itself. Muslims are humans and make mistakes and Islam is from Allah (the Almighty God) and it is perfect."

Strictly speaking, Islam and Muslims are two distinct entities. If a Muslim is involved in terrorism or any other crime, then he or she is acting contrary to the guidance of Islam, and the religion cannot be blamed for his/her actions.

Two studies were carried out on Muslim terrorists in Europe, one in the UK and the other in France. These studies found little connection between religious piety and terrorism. The first of these, a "restricted" report of hundreds of case studies by the UK domestic counter-intelligence agency MI5, concluded:

"Far from being religious zealots, a large number of those involved in terrorism do not practise their faith regularly. Many lack religious literacy and could actually be regarded as religious novices. Very few have been brought up in strongly religious households, and there is a higher than average proportion of converts. Some are involved in drug-taking, drinking alcohol and visiting prostitutes. MI5 says there is evidence that a well-established religious identity actually protects against violent radicalisation." [13]

The second study, a 2015 "general portrait" by Olivier Roy of "the conditions and circumstances" under which people living in France become "Islamic radicals" (terrorists or would-be terrorists) found radicalisation was not an "uprising of a Muslim community that is victim to poverty and racism: only young people join, including converts". [14]

Or as another observer described it: "the large majority of French jihadists are second-generation Muslims who, unlike their parents, speak French, grew up with little to no contact with mosques or Muslim organizations, and before their conversions drank, took drugs, and had girlfriends. They are estranged from their parents and don't know where to fit in. Or they are recent converts, largely from rural areas and many from divorced families. Why is that, Roy asks? If Islam or social conditions are essentially to blame for breeding terrorism, why do such structural problems affect only this very narrowly defined group? Why does it not attract first- or third-generation French Muslims, or those whose Islamic culture is the deepest? And why does its appeal extend to children of the successful middle class? His answer: jihadism is a nihilistic generational revolt, not a religiously inspired utopianism." [15]

Having mentioned these two studies, I must add that it is possible for a person who appears to be a practising Muslim to display violent behaviour due to a lack of knowledge, misunderstanding, or disregard of the teachings of Islam or some hidden agenda.

Tehrik-i-Taliban-Pakistan (TTP) is an anti-Pakistan terrorist organization that has carried out numerous terrorist attacks in Pakistan, claiming to be religiously motivated. The TTP spokesperson Ehsanullah Ehsan surrendered to the Pakistan Army at the Pakistan Afghanistan border during a military operation against terrorists. Following are some portions of his confessional statement that was published by the Pakistan Army Inter Services Public Relations (ISPR) in April 2017:

"I joined the TTP in 2008, when I was a college student".

"I have seen a lot in my nine years with TTP. <u>These people misled people in the name of Islam</u>, especially the youth, for their own ends,"

"They themselves could not come up to the standards they championed for others. A particular group is responsible for misleading people, kidnapping them and extorting them for money, and murdering innocents. These people are behind the bombing attacks in different places; attacking schools, colleges and universities. <u>This is not what Islam teaches us</u>."

"When the operation in Waziristan kicked off, these people started fighting within themselves for more power and leadership."

"After Hakimullah was killed, a new succession struggle kicked off."

"A campaign was kicked off in support of Omar Khalid Khorasani, Sajna and Mullah Fazlullah. Everyone wanted power, so a shura (consultative body) decided that there would be a draw of names for who would be leader. This is how Mullah Fazlullah was elected leader of the TTP."

"What can you expect from a leader who was nominated through a lucky draw? And what can you expect from Fazlullah, who married his mentor's daughter by force and took her away."

"After the operation in North Waziristan, we fled to Afghanistan. Over there, we established and developed contacts with India and RAW [India's spy agency]."

"They [the TTP leadership] got their [Indian] support, their funding and took money for every activity they did. They pushed the TTP soldiers on the frontlines to fight against the Pakistan Army and went into hiding themselves."

"When they started taking help from India and RAW, I told Khorasani that we're supporting the kuffar [non-believers] and helping them kill our own people in our own country."

"He [Khorasani] said: 'Even if Israel wants to fund me to destabilise Pakistan, I will not hesitate to take their help'."

"At that point, I had figured out that the TTP was functioning according to some sort of agenda that served the self-interest of its leaders."

"These [terrorist] organizations have established committees in Afghanistan through which they communicate and coordinate with RAW. The Indians had given them special visas to help them move around Afghanistan with ease. In Afghanistan, these visas function like Pakistani ID cards."

"Without these documents, it is very difficult for terrorists to move around Afghanistan considering the security situation in that country."

"These [terrorists] used to keep in contact with Afghan and Indian security forces before they moved anywhere in the country. They used to grant them passage and guide their infiltration attempts into Pakistan."

"Pakistan Army has destroyed several Jamaat-ul-Ahrar camps in Afghan territory and killed many of their commandoes in its ongoing operation. Due to this, they've had to flee the area and abandon their headquarters. Due to this, the morale of their fighters and their senior leadership has been shaken."

"There are people in those camps who have had enough; who want to quit. I want to send out a message to them." "Adopt the path of peace, and come back to a life of tranquility."

"When these people stopped getting airtime in media to the ongoing operations, they turned to social media to rope in young, innocent minds." [16]

Reading Ehsanullah Ehsan's confessional statement, it is easy to see how distant their actions are from the true teachings of Islam. Those responsible themselves know this. They brainwash young boys into carrying out suicide bombings across Pakistan.

Most of their suicide bombers are teenagers who are made to believe they will go straight to Paradise after their suicide bombing. Many of them were not even able to answer basic questions about Islam upon their capture.

Ehsanullah Ehsan's confessional statement also reveals who is supporting them and who has launched asymmetrical warfare against Pakistan. What a dirty game being played in the name of Islam!

Slain Tehreek-e-Taliban Pakistan (TTP) leader Hakimullah Mehsud's arrested aide Latif Mehsud also made similar disclosures. The United States handed him over to Pakistan in 2014 after his arrest in Afghanistan. In his statement, Mehsud also revealed that the Indian intelligence agency RAW and Afghan intelligence agency jointly direct terrorism in Pakistan through the TTP. Latif Mehsud further mentioned that he used to call the relatives of those kidnapped by the TTP. He said that he came to some realization upon reading the Quran when he was in jail. [17]

Though involved in terrorism in the name of Islam, he had not read the Holy Quran prior to his arrest. After reading the Quran in jail he realized his errors. The point to note here is who is supporting these acts. Dirty politics! Simply claiming the name of Islam does not make one a pious Muslim. Actions speak louder than words.

MISQUOTING SACRED TEXTS

One thing common between Muslim terrorists declaring religious motivation and non-Muslim adversaries of Islam is that both groups find the roots of terrorism in the Holy Quran and other sacred Islamic texts. However, this does not reflect the beliefs of the vast majority of Muslims throughout the world. As someone rightly pointed out, "The Quran has been around 1400 years, but 'Islamic' terrorism is only 20 years old phenomenon. Are you really that dumb to think the problem is Islam?" "Did Muslims just suddenly discover the Quran now or do you think there may be a complexity of social/psychological/political forces at play?"

Donald Holbrook, a Research Fellow at the Centre for the Study of Terrorism and Political Violence UK, analyzed a sample of 30 works by terrorist propagandists.

He found several passages of the Quran exploited and distorted to suit their objectives. According to him, the most quoted verses of the Quran are: An-Nisa (4:74–75) quoted most frequently; other popular passages are At-Taubah (9:13–15, 38–39, 111) and Al-Baqarah (2:190–191, 216). Holbrook argues that violent terrorists are 'shamelessly' selective in order to serve their propaganda objectives.

One cannot deny the fact that like many other topics concerning human life, the Holy Quran has several verses that address the subject of war. The following two examples from the verses referenced above by Mr. Donald Holbrook also talk about war:

"What has happened to you that you do not fight in the way of Allah, and for the oppressed among men, women and children who say, Our Lord, take us out from this town whose people are cruel, and make for us a supporter from Your own, and make for us a helper from Your own. (Surah An-Nisa, Chapter 4, Ayat 75)

"Fight in the way of Allah against those who fight you, and do not transgress. Verily, Allah does not like the transgressors." (Surah Al-Baqarah, Chapter 2, Ayat 190)

These verses of the Quran, along with a number of other such verses, are not in any way justifying terrorism but are referring to wars that are occasionally fought among nations. Islam acknowledges the existence of wars, considering them inevitable for sovereign nations, but attaches to them principles of justice and morality through delineating clear limits. As will be later discussed in Chapter 7 of this book, Islam has mandated a code of conduct to follow during these wars in order to minimize violence. From an Islamic lens, wars without any checks and balances are considered barbarism.

In several places, the Holy Quran instructs not engaging in unnecessary warfare. For example, according to the Quran, "Allah does not forbid you as regards those who did not fight you on account of faith, and did not expel you from your homes, that you do good to them, and deal justly with them. Surely Allah loves those who maintain justice." (Surah Al-Mumtahina, Chapter 60, Ayat 8)

Human life is sacred and therefore Islam does not approve unnecessary bloodshed.

The Holy Quran speaks a great deal about the sanctity of human life, for example the Quran says, "For this reason, We decreed for the children of Israel that whoever kills a person not in retaliation for a person killed, nor (as a punishment) for spreading disorder on the earth, is as if he has killed the whole of humankind, and whoever saves the life of a person is as if he has saved the life of the whole of humankind. Certainly, Our messengers have come to them with clear signs. Then, after all that, many of them are there to commit excesses on the earth." (Surah Al-Maida, Chapter 5, Ayat 32)

Islam not only sanctifies human life but also places serious emphasis on the gentle treatment of animals, for example: Prophet Muhammad (S.A.W.W) informed, "A woman was punished because she imprisoned a cat until it died. On account of this, she was doomed to Hell. While she imprisoned it, she did not give the cat food or drink, nor did she free it to eat the insects of the earth." (Reported in Sahih Bukhari and Sahih Muslim)

Prophet Muhammad (S.A.W.W) was asked, "Messenger of God, are we rewarded for kindness towards animals?" The Prophet replied, "There is a reward for kindness to every living animal or human." (Reported in Sahih Bukhari and Sahih Muslim)

There are certain principles applied by Muslim scholars for understanding the Holy Quran. One of these principles is that a Quranic verse (known as ayah) should be read (a) in the context of the surrounding verses, not in isolation, (b) in the context of its revelation, which may be found in the Hadith collections, and (c) in the context of the whole Quran. A fourth requirement is to study the words, terms, and phrases used, and as understood by the Companions of the Prophet (S.A.W.W) and the following two generations.

Another aspect of understanding the verses of the Quran is the time frame for the application of their meaning. A verse or a passage may have a special meaning for the particular time of revelation, which does not apply once the time has passed. Or a verse or a passage may have a general meaning intended for all times to come.

For the common person this simply means referring to the various commentaries of the Quran from the classical period to see how a given verse or passage was explained and understood.

Not knowing Arabic is not an excuse because in the 20th century a few commentaries of the Quran in the English language have emerged, and these writers have summed up earlier commentators.

These days, we find it increasingly common for people to misquote verses of the Quran, or narrations of Prophet Muhammad (S.A.W.W), in order to support their twisted representations of Islam as a hostile and violent religion. The majority of the verses are either mistranslated, quoted out of context, or misunderstood due to a lack of basic knowledge. Those who quote various verses of the Quran with the aim of criticism do not meet any of the aforementioned requirements, yet they interpret verses according to their whims and fancy.

I am concluding this chapter by quoting some notable statements made by Justice Haddon-Cave of the UK during his handing Ahmed Hassan, the Parsons Green tube bomber, a minimum term of 34 years imprisonment for the "death and carnage" he desired.

The teenager was told by Justice Haddon-Cave that he had "violated Islam" as he was jailed for life for launching a terror attack on the London Underground, "you have violated the Quran and Islam with your actions, as well as the law of all civilised people". "It is to be hoped that you will come to realise this one day." Justice Haddon-Cave said the Quran was a "book of peace" and noted its teachings forbidding terrorism and crime, adding: "You will have plenty of time to study the Quran in prison in the years to come." [18]

Chapter 4

POLITICAL CONNECTION

"Terrorism cannot be isolated from its political, historical, and even social context."

(**Zbigniew Brzezinski**, *Polish-American diplomat & political scientist*) [1]

As mentioned earlier in Chapter 2, most definitions of terrorism encompass the motive of political gains which is prevalent even among terrorists claiming to be religiously motived. Some writers go as far to suggest that terrorism is the product of 'politics'. For example, in his article 'It's not the religion that creates terrorists, it's the politics' Mr. Giles Fraser mentions, "The radicalisation hypothesis steers us away from the real causes of terrorism – and enables the west to maintain its denial about a role in helping create it." [2]

This chapter discusses some of the political aspects of global extremism and terrorism. The chapter also addresses the pivotal role of media in the war against terrorism and the rise of hate crimes against Muslims.

POLITICAL CONTEXT

According to a CNN report dated June 30, 2005: "After studying 315 suicide attacks from 1981-2004, the University of Chicago political science professor concludes that suicide bombers' actions stem from logical military strategies, not their religion -- and especially not Islam.

While American news-watchers may hear more about Israel and Iraq, Pape calls the Tamil Tigers the leading purveyors of suicide attacks over the last two decades -- until now. An adamantly secular group with Hindu roots, the Tamil Tigers are engaged in a struggle for independence and power with the Sri Lankan government.

So what is the suicide bomber's main rationale? It is that the attacks work, Pape found.

'What nearly all suicide terrorist attacks have in common is a specific secular and strategic goal: to compel modern democracies to withdraw military forces from territory that the terrorists consider to be their homeland.'

Which means, in the case of al Qaeda and like-minded groups, getting the United States out of the Arabian Peninsula and Iraq." [3]

In a scholarly article written for Foreign Affairs in 2007, Tony Blair (ex-Prime Minister of UK), who was soon to step down as prime minister, outlined his views on terrorism in the wake of events that followed 9/11. According to Mr. Blair:

"The roots of the current wave of global terrorism and extremism are deep. They reach down through decades of alienation, victimhood, and political oppression in the Arab and Muslim world. Yet such terrorism is not and never has been inevitable …

Terrorism did not begin on the streets of New York [on 9/11]. Many more had already died, not just in acts of terrorism against Western interests but in political insurrection and turmoil around the world. Its victims are to be found in the recent history of many lands: India, Indonesia, Kenya, Libya, Pakistan, Russia, Saudi Arabia, Yemen, and countless more. More than 100,000 died in Algeria. In Chechnya and Kashmir, political causes that could have been resolved became brutally incapable of resolution under the pressure of terrorism.

Today, in 30 or 40 countries, terrorists are plotting action loosely linked with this ideology. Although the active cadres of terrorists are relatively small, they exploit a far wider sense of alienation in the Arab and Muslim world … The struggle against terrorism in Madrid, or London, or Paris is the same as the struggle against the terrorist acts of Hezbollah in Lebanon, or Palestinian Islamic Jihad in the Palestinian territories, or rejectionist groups in Iraq. The murder of the innocent in Beslan is part of the same ideology that takes innocent lives in Libya, Saudi Arabia, or Yemen." [4]

Even Osama Bin Laden (former leader of Al-Qaeda) included political reasons in his 2002 broadcast, while laying out his organization's principle objectives.

He said, "Why should fear, killing, destruction, displacement, orphaning and widowing continue to be our lot, while security, stability and happiness be your lot [the West led by the US]? This is unfair. It is time that we get even. You will be killed just as you kill, and will be bombed just as you bomb. And expect more that will further distress you." [5]

When asked 'What do you seek?' during his 1998 interview to Al-Jazeera, Osama Bin Laden replied, "What I seek is what is right for any living being. We demand that our land be liberated from enemies. That our lands be liberated from the Americans. These living beings have been given an inner sense that rejects any intrusions [of their lands] by outsiders. Let us take an example of poultry. Let us look at a chicken, for example. If an armed person was to enter a chicken's home with the aim of inflicting harm to it, the chicken would automatically fight back." [6]

While I was still writing this book, another development occurred that may add more fuel to the fire of extremism. US president Donald Trump formally recognized Jerusalem as Israel's capital where he has decided to move the US embassy. The diplomatic status of Jerusalem is one of the world's thorniest issues. Such decisions may be detrimental to world peace. The Arab League's Secretary-General Ahmed Aboul Gheit has commented on this, "We say very clearly that taking such action is not justified ... It will not serve peace or stability, but will fuel extremism and result to violence." [7]

According to a December 2017 Guardian report: "The United Nations general assembly has delivered a stinging rebuke to Donald Trump, voting by a huge majority to reject his unilateral recognition of Jerusalem as Israel's capital. The vote came after a redoubling of threats by Nikki Haley, the US ambassador to the UN, who said that Washington would remember which countries 'disrespected' America by voting against it. Despite the warning, 128 members voted on Thursday in favour of the resolution supporting the longstanding international consensus that the status of Jerusalem – which is claimed as a capital by both Israel and the Palestinians – can only be settled as an agreed final issue in a peace deal."

"Countries which voted for the resolution included major recipients of US aid such as Egypt, Afghanistan and Iraq. ...only nine states – including the United States and Israel –voted against the resolution. The other countries which supported Washington were Togo, Micronesia, Nauru, Palau, Marshall Islands, Guatemala and Honduras."[8]

The aforementioned quotations and facts inform us of the political bases of terrorism. In the global fight against terrorism, it is therefore of utmost importance that long standing political issues be resolved amicably among nations. The United Nations Organization (UNO) provides an excellent platform for this purpose which can be made more effective. Similarly, no new issues should be created by political powers including global 'superpowers'. Otherwise terrorism may thrive and continue to exist as it is sometimes referred to as being 'a weapon of the weak'. I sincerely hope this is not the case.

CRITICS OF THE WAR ON TERROR

Thus far I have discussed the political motives inciting terrorism. But many have also alluded to the political objectives embedded in the war on terror, especially after the Iraq invasion. Ben Dupre, a British author, in his book '50 Political Ideas you really need to know' writes:

"While the threat to the West posed by Islamic extremists was very real, the Western response to it betrayed insensitivity and lack of understanding. The United States blandly assumed the role of champion of freedom and democracy against a pitiless and fanatical enemy; and from this unnuanced perspective, fear and suspicion of Islamism was projected, often indiscriminately, onto Muslims and Islam as a whole. To many in the Muslim world, on the other hand, the US-led response to 9/11 looked hasty and disingenuous, and nothing that followed eased their suspicion of the West's imperialistic ambitions and less-than-pure motives, particularly with respect to its oil interests."[9]

Noam Chomsky is an eminent American psychologist and philosopher. Since the Vietnam War in the 1960's, he has also been a major political figure and fierce critic of US foreign policy. His following views on Iraq were equally forceful:

"Bush, Dick Cheney, Donald Rumsfeld and company are committed to an 'imperial ambition', as G. John Ikenberry wrote in the September/October issue of Foreign Affairs – 'a unipolar world in which the United States has no peer competitor' and in which 'no state or coalition could ever challenge it as global leader, protector and enforcer'.

That ambition surely includes much expanded control over Persian Gulf resources and military bases to impose a preferred form of order in the region.

Even before the administration began beating the war drums against Iraq, there were plenty of warnings that U.S. adventurism would lead to proliferation of weapons of mass destruction, as well as terror, for deterrence or revenge.

Right now, Washington is teaching the world a dangerous lesson: If you want to defend yourself from us, you had better mimic North Korea and pose a credible threat. Otherwise we will demolish you.

There is good reason to believe that the war with Iraq is intended, in part, to demonstrate what lies ahead when the empire decides to strike a blow – though 'war' is hardly the proper term, given the gross mismatch of forces.

... The potential disasters are among the many reasons why decent human beings do not contemplate the threat or use of violence, whether in personal life or international affairs, unless reasons have been offered that have overwhelming force. And surely nothing remotely like that justification has come forward." [10]

Immediately after 9/11, all state leaders and the major part of the general populace sympathized with the US and supported the Bush administration in its response to the terrorist threat and its declaration of a 'war on terror'. This mood, however, began to disperse in 2002. According to Paul Rogers of the University of Bradford the reason was:

"... it became apparent that the war on terror's deeper agenda was largely driven by the desire to facilitate what the more fervent neoconservative supporters of the Bush administration were calling a 'new American century'."

"The Washington view was that it was essential to maintain control of the world. Its model was impelled by a unilateralist stance owing much to a central tenet of the neocon outlook: what is good for the White House is good for the world." [11]

Zbigniew Brzezinski had been the National Security Advisor to US President Jimmy Carter. His critical views about the 'war on terror' can be inferred from his following statement:

"Constant reference to a 'war on terror' did accomplish one major objective. It stimulated the emergence of a culture of fear. Fear obscures reason, intensifies emotions and makes it easier for demagogic politicians to mobilize the public on behalf of the policies they want to pursue. The war of choice in Iraq could never have gained the congressional support it got without the psychological linkage between the shock of 9/11 and the postulated existence of Iraqi weapons of mass destruction. Support for President Bush in the 2004 elections was also mobilized in part by the notion that 'a nation at war' does not change its commander in chief midstream. The sense of a pervasive but otherwise imprecise danger was thus channeled in a politically expedient direction by the mobilizing appeal of being 'at war'." [12]

THE MAKING OF AL-QAEDA AND ISIS

I must commend Ms. Hillary Clinton who had the guts to make the following statements during a two-day continuous congressional hearing on the Obama administration's foreign policy:

"Let's remember here... the people we are fighting today we funded them twenty years ago... and we did it because we were locked in a struggle with the Soviet Union."

"They invaded Afghanistan... and we did not want to see them control Central Asia and we went to work... and it was President Reagan in partnership with Congress led by Democrats who said you know what it sounds like a pretty good idea... let's deal with the ISI (Intelligence agency in Pakistan) and the Pakistan military and let's go recruit these mujahideen (Muslim fighters)."

"And great, let them come from Saudi Arabia and other countries, importing their Wahabi brand of Islam so that we can go beat the Soviet Union."

"And guess what ... they (Soviets) retreated ... they lost billions of dollars and it led to the collapse of the Soviet Union."

"So there is a very strong argument which is... it wasn't a bad investment in terms of Soviet Union but let's be careful with what we sow... because we will harvest."

"So we then left Pakistan ... We said okay fine you deal with the Stingers that we left all over your country... you deal with the mines that are along the border and... by the way we don't want to have anything to do with you... in fact we're sanctioning you... So we stopped dealing with the Pakistani military and with ISI and we now are making up for a lot of lost time." [13]

Many people, including those in the West, have criticized US policies in the Middle East which according to them are at least partially, if not directly, responsible for the emergence of ISIS. The group's roots are in the Sunni group Al-Qaeda in Iraq (AQI), which was created in 2004 by Jordanian Islamist Abu Musab al-Zarqawi. The AQI was a major player in the insurgency against US-led forces that toppled Saddam Hussein in 2003.

Graham Fuller, an author and former CIA officer, in an interview while responding to the question 'How do you think ISIS was born?, said: "I think the United States is one of the key creators of this organization. The United States did not plan the formation of ISIS, but its destructive interventions in the Middle East and the war in Iraq were the basic causes of the birth of ISIS. You will remember that that the starting point of this organization was to protest the US invasion of Iraq. In those days it was supported by many non-Islamist Sunnis as well because of their opposition to the Iraq's occupation. I think even today ISIS [now the Islamic State] is supported by many Sunnis who feel isolated by the Shiite government in Baghdad. ISIS was benefiting from the Shiite agenda of the [former Prime Minister Nouri al-Maliki] government. I hope with the departure of Maliki and his replacement by someone who will watch out for Sunni-Shiite balance, polarization in Iraq will diminish. This is the only way to get rid of ISIS, never militarily." [14]

Even President Donald Trump can be seen in a YouTube video openly condemning the Obama administration for the creation of ISIS. [15] According to a CNN report: "Plenty has been said about Donald Trump calling President Barack Obama the 'founder of ISIS.' The GOP presidential candidate added to the conversation himself on Friday, tweeting that he was being sarcastic when he made the remarks. A day earlier, he told a radio host that Obama deserves blame for the Muslim terror group's rise because of the US military withdrawal from Iraq in 2011, which left a power vacuum for the terror group to exploit." [16]

Some people have even gone to the extreme of blaming the US of colluding with ISIS. The former President of Afghanistan Hamid Karzai is one such example. According to an Aljazeera report:

"Hamid Karzai, the former president of Afghanistan, has accused the US of working with the Islamic State of Iraq and the Levant (ISIL) group in his country.

In an exclusive interview with Al Jazeera's UpFront aired on Friday, Karzai said the US government had allowed ISIL, also known as ISIS, to flourish inside Afghanistan.

'In my view under the full presence, surveillance, military, political, intelligence, Daesh [ISIL] has emerged,' he said.

'And for two years the Afghan people came, cried loud about their suffering, of violations. Nothing was done.'

Karzai said the US administration of President Donald Trump used ISIL as an excuse to drop a massive bomb on Afghanistan in April 2017.

'And the next day, Daesh takes the next district in Afghanistan,' he said referring to the Arabic name of the armed group.

'That proves to us that there is a hand in it and that hand can be no one else but them [the US] in Afghanistan.' [17]

Most people, however, believe that it was the deeply misguided policies of the US which supported the formation of ISIS, rather than it having a direct hand in its creation. Noam Chomsky also shares this view regarding the genesis of ISIS. [18]

MEDIA AND THE SELECTIVE USE OF TERMS

The media has become an integral part of society. For the majority of the population, it is now the television, newspapers and internet that supply primary information regarding political events. Thus, the media plays a distinctive role in framing public opinion and this is true as well about war and terror.

Some people may believe that the media provides an impartial account of events. However, the truth is that the media is often guilty of partiality. According to the Open University's (UK) training manual on 'Politics, Media and War: 9/11 and its aftermaths':

"While the media often appear to provide a clear and impartial analysis, it is first important to recognise that media production is rarely a politically neutral process.

The information or images offered up by the media do not simply mirror some 'objective' or 'factual' reality that exists 'out there', but tend to be selected and shaped (explicitly or implicitly) in ways that support the world-views or interests of the people and organisation(s) making the media text.

This is not to say that the events portrayed in, say, news and current affairs are simply works of fiction invented by journalists, but rather to suggest that what is often authoritatively presented as real, factual and objective is actually constructed through a process of selection. This process, when examined, can often reveal how embedded social and political values and organisational processes can work to produce different 'realities' of any given situation." [19]

Since September 11, 2001, the world's attention has largely been focused on the violence of Islamic terrorism. The continuation of terrorist activities since 9/11, and the selective use of the term 'terrorism' by Western media and politicians reserved for Muslims, have created an atmosphere of Islamophobia. As a result, the Muslim community at large, and especially those seen as more practicing, have come under heavy suspicion in the West.

Such biased reporting by the media is very much felt by Muslims all over the world. This discontent has been repeatedly expressed in discussions and writings.

The following is an excerpt of an article by a Muslim writer that criticizes the selective use of the term terrorism:

"Mark Anthony Conditt, a 23-year-old white man who self-identified as conservative in a 2012 blog, killed two people in Austin with bombs, apparently targeted for their race, and injured many others. He then blew himself up in an actual suicide bombing, injuring a police officer in the process.

But he's not being called a terrorist.

If he were Muslim, that label would be a given, long before any evidence was provided of ideological motives. And with him, an entire community would face trial.

For me as a visible Muslim, and for many other members of marginalized communities, every act of violence is a double calamity: We mourn the loss of life and grieve for the victims' families. We then brace ourselves for the public punishment and collective blame for a crime we didn't commit if the perpetrator happens to share a dimension of our identity.

In America, this dual trauma after a national tragedy is a burden exclusive to communities of color. Though white men carry out the majority of mass shootings and ideologically motivated violence, white people don't face collective criminalization when 'one of them' behaves badly.

We don't change laws, implement more surveillance, reform curriculum, demand condemnations or ask what the assailant heard in his church's last sermon. We treat the incident as isolated, an aberration, something we could not have prevented or predicted, and most certainly not a reflection on the shooter's culture, race or religion more broadly.

This double standard in perception is more than a regrettable media bias; it provides public cover for targeted state oppression" [20]

Now, the question arises that why does the media not maintain neutrality? This point is well explained by E.S Herman and N. Chomsky in their book 'Manufacturing Consent: the political economy of the mass media' in the following words:

"The mass media are drawn into a symbiotic relationship with powerful sources of information by economic necessity and reciprocity of interest. The media need a steady, reliable flow of the raw material of news. They have daily news demands and imperative news schedules that they must meet. They cannot afford to have reporters and cameras at all places where important stones may break. Economics dictates that they concentrate their resources where significant news often occurs, where important rumors and leaks abound, and where regular press conferences are held. The White House, the Pentagon, and the State Department, in Washington, D.C., are central nodes of such news activity. On a local basis, city hall and the police department are the subject of regular news 'beats' for reporters. Business corporations and trade groups are also regular and credible purveyors of stories deemed newsworthy. These bureaucracies turn out a large volume of material that meets the demands of news organizations for reliable, scheduled flows. Mark Fishman calls this 'the principle of bureaucratic affinity: only other bureaucracies can satisfy the input needs of a news bureaucracy.'

Government and corporate sources also have the great merit of being recognizable and credible by their status and prestige. This is important to the mass media. As Fishman notes,

Newsworkers are predisposed to treat bureaucratic accounts as factual because news personnel participate in upholding a normative order of authorized knowers in the society. Reporters operate with the attitude that officials ought to know what it is their job to know.... In particular, a newsworker will recognize an official's claim to knowledge not merely as a claim, but as a credible, competent piece of knowledge. This amounts to a moral division of labor; officials have and give the facts; reporters merely get them.

Another reason for the heavy weight given to official sources is that the mass media claim to be 'objective' dispensers of the news. Partly to maintain the image of objectivity, but also to protect themselves from criticisms of bias and the threat of libel suits, they need material that can be portrayed as presumptively accurate. This is also partly a matter of cost: taking information from sources that may be presumed credible reduces investigative expense, whereas material from sources that are not prima facie credible, or that will elicit criticism and threats, requires careful checking and costly research."

"To consolidate their preeminent position as sources, government and business-news promoters go to great pains to make things easy for news organizations. They provide the media organizations with facilities in which to gather; they give journalists advance copies of speeches and forthcoming reports; they schedule press conferences at hours well-geared to news deadlines they write press releases in usable language; and they carefully organize their press conferences and 'photo opportunity' sessions. It is the job of news officers 'to meet the journalist's scheduled needs with material that their beat agency has generated at its own pace.'

In effect, the large bureaucracies of the powerful subsidize the mass media, and gain special access by their contribution to reducing the media's costs of acquiring the raw materials of, and producing, news. The large entities that provide this subsidy become 'routine' news sources and have privileged access to the gates. Non-routine sources must struggle for access, and may be ignored by the arbitrary decision of the gatekeepers. It should also be noted that in the case of the largesse of the Pentagon and the State Department's Office of Public Diplomacy, the subsidy is at the taxpayers' expense, so that, in effect, the citizenry pays to be propagandized in the interest of powerful groups such as military contractors and other sponsors of state terrorism.

Because of their services, continuous contact on the beat, and mutual dependency, the powerful can use personal relationships, threats, and rewards to further influence and coerce the media. The media may feel obligated to carry extremely dubious stories and mute criticism in order not to offend their sources and disturb a close relationship. It is very difficult to call authorities on whom one depends for daily news liars, even if they tell whoppers. Critical sources may be avoided not only because of their lesser availability and higher cost of establishing credibility, but also because the primary sources may be offended and may even threaten the media using them.

The relation between power and sourcing extends beyond official and corporate provision of day-to-day news to shaping the supply of 'experts.' The dominance of official sources is weakened by the existence of highly respectable unofficial sources that give dissident views with great authority."

"This problem is alleviated by 'co-opting the experts' — i.e., putting them on the payroll as consultants, funding their research, and organizing think tanks that will hire them directly and help disseminate their messages. In this way bias may be structured, and the supply of experts may be skewed in the direction desired by the government and 'the market.' As Henry Kissinger has pointed out, in this 'age of the expert,' the 'constituency' of the expert is 'those who have a vested interest in commonly held opinions; elaborating and defining its consensus at a high level has, after all, made him an expert.' It is therefore appropriate that this restructuring has taken place to allow the commonly held opinions (meaning those that are functional for elite interests) to continue to prevail." [21]

RISE IN HATE CRIMES AGAINST MUSLIMS

With the recent climate of Islamophobia, there has been an increase in hate crimes against Muslims. While discussing this prevailing problem in the USA, an NBC News article published on September 11, 2016, reported, "Anti-Muslim hate crimes are approximately five times more frequent than they were before 2001, according to the FBI. The past year has been particularly brutal, especially in the aftermath of Islamic State-claimed attacks in Europe and the San Bernardino shootings last December carried out by a Muslim husband and wife. More reports of mosque vandalism and attacks against those believed to be Muslim surfaced. Anti-Muslim rhetoric has also been given an enormous boost of pseudo-credibility and prominence by Republican presidential nominee Donald Trump." [22]

These hate crimes have gone to an extreme in recent times. One example is of the 'Punish a Muslim Day' letters that were sent across the UK by unknown culprits, provoking people to attack Muslims on a certain day. According to a newspaper's March, 2018 report:

"The anonymous letters arrived this weekend in plain white envelopes with second-class stamps, and were sent to people in at least six communities in England. Inside was a message so hateful that it sent out ripples of alarm and prompted a national counterterrorism investigation."

"The message said that April 3 would be 'Punish a Muslim Day,' and that points would be awarded for acts of violence: 25 points for pulling off a woman's head scarf, 500 points for murdering a Muslim and 1,000 for bombing a mosque." [23]

Such hate crimes targeting a particular community are as hideous as acts of terrorism and should be condemned alongside.

Chapter 5

ISLAM AND EXTREMISM

"To go beyond the bounds of moderation is to outrage humanity."

(Blaise Pascal, French mathematician, philosopher & physicist) [1]

As mentioned earlier in Chapter 2 of this book, 'extremism' is one among a number of frequented terms of the post 9/11 era. It is typically used in a religious or political sense to refer to an ideology that is considered, either by the speaker or by some implied shared social consensus, to be far outside the acceptable mainstream attitudes or norms of society. As such, 'extremism' is often interchangeably used with 'terrorism'.

Reflecting popular usage, some definitions of extremism narrow their focus only on the holding of extreme 'political' or 'religious' views'. Others are more expansive, incorporating any extreme idea whether it be religious, political, social, or economic. The Merriam Webster Dictionary proposes this more inclusive view by defining extremism as 'the quality or state of being extreme'. [2]

Unlike other religions, Islam provides guidance in religious matters as well as secular matters that are normally considered to be outside religious jurisdiction. The guidance of Islam encompasses all facets of human life, whether spiritual or economic, political or social, leaving no aspect untouched. The level of detail may however vary from subject to subject. In some areas Islam only provides a few guiding principles, whereas detailed instructions are provided in many other areas. That is why Islam is sometimes referred to as a complete system of life.

The question then naturally arises whether this system is one that is extreme or moderate? Is Islam a progressive religion or a fanatical, regressive regime? Does Islam want its adherents to return to the medieval ages? Does Islam oppose modern scientific developments or does it promote them?

These are the kinds of questions that are explored in this chapter.

ISLAM – A MODERATE SYSTEM

The opposite of 'extremism' is 'moderation' which implies, by its very definition, that something is not extreme if it is proved to be moderate. Throughout time, human beings have taken many extreme positions in multiple spheres of human activity. For the sake of analysis, I will classify the various spheres of human activity into the following four categories, 1) religious or spiritual system, 2) social system, 3) economic system, and 4) political system. Extreme positions have been taken with respect to all four of these areas. If we were to draw a continuum of the different views and tendencies belonging to these categories, we would see extreme positions at the two ends and moderate ones inclining towards the center. Human endeavors can miss the point of justice, or what can alternatively be called the point of moderation, between the extremes, and this has been a recurring cause of suffering especially for the common man.

The following analysis demonstrates that the teachings and guidance of Islam are always set apart from the extreme positions that have been taken in these four spheres of human activity, embodying a moderate balance. For this analysis I will be making reference to Islamic teachings instead of current Muslim practices, which may or may not be fully aligned with the teachings of Islam.

Religious or spiritual system:

With respect to one's religious/spiritual life, we see two extreme positions, <u>monasticism</u> and <u>materialism</u>. The first extreme of monasticism tends to kills one's natural physical desires while the other extreme of pure materialism focuses only on materialistic desires, negating the demands of the spirit all together. We find varying attempts at reconciling the conflict of body and soul in human history.

Most people incline towards a sensate outlook in life, culminating in degrees of materialism and hedonism, often depriving themselves of a moral, ethical, and spiritual outlook on individual as well as collective matters. This is one extreme.

On the other hand, certain people who wanted to follow the path of moral and spiritual excellence invented such ascetic practices and spiritual exercises that it killed their natural physical desires.

They migrated to solitary places like forests and mountains in search of hideouts where they would be least disturbed by the hustle and bustle of the world. They would busy themselves with spiritual practices, prolonged hunger and thirst, and nose-gazing meditations, so much so that they would virtually become 'noble outcasts' of this world.

Islam is far away from both extremes; it prescribes a system which develops a moral and spiritual personality while remaining practically engaged in everyday life. Islam requires that people turn to the path which leads to Allah's Good Pleasure. Allah s.w.t says in the Holy Quran, "The (material) things which ye are given are but the conveniences of this life and the glitter thereof; but that which is with Allah is better and more enduring: will ye not then be wise?" (Surah Al-Qasas, Chapter 28, Ayat 60) Prophet Muhammad (S.A.W.W) said, "By Allah! The similitude of this world compared with the Hereafter is just like one of you dipping his finger in the ocean and then looking at it to see how much (water) it has brought out with it." (Sahih Muslim)

But this wisdom neither means a gloomy, starved existence nor perpetual formal prayers in isolation. Rather one serves Allah through leading a pure, obedient life within the turmoil of this world. This connection to the realities of worldly life was lost, or at least not fostered by monastic institutions. This world also requires courage, resistance to evil, firmness, and law and discipline to enforce justice among the people. It requires that people mingle with people, so that they can uphold the standard of truth, against odds if necessary. These qualities were lost in Monasticism.

There is an excellent prayer mentioned in the Holy Quran that depicts this balanced approach. The prayer is: "...Our Lord, give us good in this world and good in the Hereafter, and save us from the punishment of Fire." (Surah Baqarah, Chapter 2, Ayat 201).

Even with respect to the performance of prayer, the Quran prescribes a middle path, for example the Quran says, "... Do not be (too) loud in your Salah (prayers), nor be (too) low in it, and seek a way in between." (Surah Bani Israel, Chapter 17, Ayat 110)

The tendency of Monasticism was also displayed by some early Muslims and thereon afterwards. Prophet Muhammad (S.A.W.W) always discouraged such tendencies.

For example, a group of three men came to the houses of the wives of the Prophet Muhammad (S.A.W.W) asking how the Prophet (S.A.W.W) worshipped (Allah), and when they were informed about that, they considered their worship insufficient and said, "Where are we from the Prophet as his past and future sins have been forgiven." Then one of them said, "I will offer the prayer throughout the night forever." The other said, "I will fast throughout the year and will not break my fast." The third said, "I will keep away from the women and will not marry forever." Allah's Apostle (S.A.W.W) came to them and said, "Are you the same people who said so-and-so? By Allah, I am more submissive to Allah and more afraid of Him than you; yet I fast and break my fast, I do sleep and I also marry women. So he who does not follow my tradition in religion, is not from me (not one of my followers)." (Sahih Bukhari)

Abdullah bin Amr (R.A.A) informed that Allah's Apostle entered upon me and said, "Have I not been informed that you offer prayer all the night and fast the whole day?" I said, "Yes." He said, "Do not do so; offer prayer at night and also sleep; fast for a few days and give up fasting for a few days because your body has a right on you, and your eye has a right on you, and your guest has a right on you, and your wife has a right on you. I hope that you will have a long life, and it is sufficient for you to fast for three days a month as the reward of a good deed, is multiplied ten times, that means, as if you fasted the whole year." I insisted (on fasting more) so I was given a hard instruction. I said, "I can do more than that (fasting)." The Prophet said, "Fast three days every week." But as I insisted (on fasting more) so I was burdened. I said, "I can fast more than that." The Prophet (S.A.W.W) said, "Fast as Allah's prophet David used to fast." I said, "How was the fasting of the prophet David?" The Prophet said, "One half of a year (i.e. he used to fast on alternate days)." (Sahih Bukhari)

Another hadith reporting this event informs that Abdullah bin Amr (R.A.A) further said, "O Allah's Apostle! I can do (fast) more than that." The Prophet (S.A.W.W) replied, "There is nothing better than that." (Sahih Bukhari)

Social system:

In the case of social systems, Islam also provides a moderate and balanced view. For example, the following verse of the Quran prescribes moderation with respect to social behavior.

"And swell not thy cheek (for pride) at men nor walk in insolence through the earth; for Allah loveth not any arrogant boaster. And be moderate in thy pace and lower thy voice; for the harshest of sounds without doubt is the braying of the ass." (Surah Luqman, Chapter 31, Ayats 18 – 19)

Take the case of an individual's freedom in society. The two extremes would be <u>absolute freedom</u> without any checks and <u>very limited or no freedom</u> for the citizens of a state. Islam steers clear of both extremes as displayed in the following analysis.

Every system is epitomized by a slogan. The slogan for Capitalism is 'Liberty / Freedom'. Liberty is a positive virtue to target, but the problem is when we try to grant perfect liberty to individuals, we lose the virtue of equality in the process. The following quotes of some notables regarding Liberty and Capitalism acknowledge this fact.

"Advocates of Capitalism are very apt to appeal to the sacred principles of liberty, which are embodied in one maxim: The fortunate must not be restrained in the exercise of tyranny over the unfortunate." (Bertrand Russell, English Logician and Philosopher 1872-1970) [3]

"When liberty comes with hands dabbled in blood it is hard to shake hands with her." (Oscar Wilde, French Philosopher and Writer, 1694-1778) [4]

On the other hand, Communist movements surfaced in many parts of the world that promulgated the concept of 'Equality'. Again, equality is a positive virtue to target, but when we forcefully pursue complete equality amongst people, it comes at the cost of liberty. As mentioned by Winston Churchill, "It is not alone that property, in all its forms, is struck at, but that liberty, in all its forms, is challenged by the fundamental conceptions of Socialism". [5]

Islam emphasizes 'Justice.' According to the Holy Quran, "Lo! Allah enjoineth justice and kindness, and giving to kinsfolk, and forbiddeth lewdness and abomination and wickedness. He exhorteth you in order that ye may take heed." (Surah An-Nahl, Chapter 16, Ayat 90).

Islam even does justice between the values of 'Liberty' and 'Equality'. Islam believes in liberty and freedom but with certain checks and balances so that equality is not totally lost in the process. The concept of freedom in a pure Capitalistic system means absolute and unrestricted freedom based on the doctrine of Laissez Faire. In the Islamic system, there is conditional freedom that is subject to two major qualifications: 1) The dictates of ethics, and 2) The interest of the community at large.

Now take the case of women. Both men and women are important segments of any society. There was a time when there were such extreme negative views about women that she was <u>not even considered a true human being with a pious soul</u>. Instead, she was deemed a source of evil and had no rights. For example, in the Roman Empire, Roman Law gave no rights to women. A woman could not be the owner of any kind of property. When Roman Civilization was at the zenith of its 'glory', a man even possessed the right to take the life of his wife.

The Greek civilization is considered the most glorious of all ancient civilizations. Under this very 'glorious' system, women were deprived of all rights and looked down upon. According to ancient Greek mythology, the very first woman was created out of the earth by Hephaestus at the request of Zeus, the king of the gods, and sent down into the world with a box containing all kinds of misery and evil. It was the intention of Zeus to punish Prometheus who had stolen fire from the heaven and bestowed it upon the mortals. The story goes that from the moment the box was opened, the world has been plagued with wickedness and sorrow. This woman was given the name of Pandora, a Greek word which originally meant 'all-giving', but which came to be synonymous with 'giver of all evils'. The box that she brought with her is called the Pandora Box.

Similarly, there was a great symposium held in France in 586 AD wherein it was settled through a proposition that the female has only been created for the service of man, and as a independent creature she has no rights and role.

This was the global social environment at the time of the advent of Islam which brought with it revolutionary teachings including those regarding the status of women.

The following guidance was revealed by Allah s.w.t in the Holy Quran regarding the relationship of husband and wife: "....they are your garments. And ye are their garments....." (Surah Al-Baqara, Chapter 2, Verse 187)

Radical feminists have now gone to another extreme of completely equating men and women. There is a particular reason behind such behaviour as mentioned by Tamara McClintock Greenberg, Psy.D., M.S., a clinical psychologist in her article 'Differences between men and women: Talking about Inequalities in the Shadow of the Feminist Movement', "Those of us in our 40's and beyond were reared in a time in which we felt we had to deny differences between the sexes. This message had a purpose. We had to justify equal rights and equal pay." [6]

According to Louann Brizendine, M.D, author of a bestselling book published in 2006 about the way in which male and female brains and bodies differ, "...pretending that women and men are the same, while doing a disservice to both men and women, ultimately hurts women." [7] Women cannot compete with men by becoming men. They are different therefore their needs are different. According to Eva Evelyn Burrows an Australian community welfare organizer, "We have to be careful in this era of radical feminism, not to emphasize an equality of the sexes that leads women to imitate men to prove their equality. To be equal does not mean you have to be the same." [8]

Islam once again demonstrates a balanced approach in this matter. While recognizing both men and women as equals as human beings, Islam prescribes differences with respect to their roles and responsibilities in a society. But a difference in roles does not mean degrading a gender. In fact, Islam strongly emphasizes the respect of women. The following sayings of Prophet Muhammad (S.A.W.W) highlight the degree to which Islam stresses the good treatment of women.

A man came to Prophet Muhammad (S.A.W.W) and said, "O Allah's Apostle! Who is more entitled to be treated with the best companionship by me?" The Prophet said, "Your mother." The man said. "Who is next?" The Prophet said, "Your mother." The man further said, "Who is next?" The Prophet said, "Your mother." The man asked for the fourth time, "Who is next?" The Prophet said, "Your father." (Reported in Sahih Bukhari)

The Prophet Mohammad (S.A.W.W) said, "Look after your mother because your Heaven lies beneath her feet". (Ibn Maja, and Nisai)

Prophet Muhammad (S.A.W.W) said, "Whoever has a girl (daughter, sister, etc) under his guardianship, and he neither buries her alive, nor treats her with contempt, nor give preference to his sons over her, Allah will admit him to Paradise." (Abu Dawood)

Instead of stringent 'equality' between the two sexes, Islam believes in the concept of 'equity'. The concept of equity abstain from forcing uniformity between the two sexes; instead it highlights and values their natural similarities and differences. Men and women are created differently and therefore their needs vary. Based on the concept of equity, these needs should be recognized and fulfilled.

A complete discussion on the topic of women and women's rights can be read in my previous book 'Women, Feminism and Islam' available at www.amazon.com. [9]

Economic system:

Any book on economics discusses a continuum of economic systems with the <u>Market economy</u> (Capitalism) on one extreme and the <u>Command economy</u> (Communism) on the other. In between these, are the mixed economies.

After experimenting with the economic extremes of pure Capitalism and pure Communism, the world has learned their bitter lessons, and the majority of countries today feature mixed economies. Over time, each country made adjustments to the workings of its economy, and this modification and tweaking is an ongoing process even today. The current trend is a steady increase in government intervention in industry and trade, thus decreasing the individual freedom.

Paul A. Samuelson was the first American to win a Nobel Prize in Economics. In his book 'Economics' he explains: "No contemporary society falls completely into either of these polar categories. Rather, all societies are mixed economies, with elements of market and command. There has never been a 100% market economy (although nineteenth-century England came close)."

"Today most decisions in the United States are made in the marketplace. But the Government plays an important role in modifying the functioning of the market; the Government sets laws and rules that regulate economic life, produces educational and police services, and regulates pollution and business. And the Soviet Union and the countries of Eastern Europe, unhappy with the performance of their command economies, are searching for their own particular brands of the mixed economy." [10]

Away from the two extremes, the economic system of Islam is a type of a mixed economy. One of the leading Islamic scholars, Mufti Muhammad Taqi Usmani explains the Islamic economic system in his words:

"Islam does not deny the market forces and market economy. Even the profit motive is acceptable to a reasonable extent. Private ownership is not totally negated. Yet, the basic difference between the Capitalist and Islamic economy is that in Secular Capitalism, the profit motive and private ownership are given unbridled power to make economic decisions. Their liberty is not controlled by any Divine Injunctions. If there are some restrictions, they are imposed by human beings and are always subject to change through democratic legislation, which accepts no authority of any super-human power. This attitude has allowed a number of practices which cause imbalances in the society. ...The evils emanating from this attitude can never be curbed unless the humanity submits to the Divine Authority and obeys its commands in any case and at every price. This is exactly what Islam does. After recognizing private ownership, profit motive, and market forces, Islam has put certain divine restrictions on the economic activities. These restrictions being imposed by Allah Almighty, Whose knowledge has no limits, cannot be removed by any human authority. All these prohibitions combined together have a cumulative effect of maintaining balance, distributive justice, and equality of opportunities." [11]

The prohibition of usury, gambling, hoarding, unlawful goods or services, short sales, and speculative transactions are some examples of Divine restrictions on the Islamic economy.

Political system:

In the political arena, once again we find a point of moderation in the guidance of Islam. One extreme the world witnessed was the system of Theocracy, for example the Christian Theocracy of medieval Europe where the words uttered by the Pope constituted law. The reaction to Theocracy resulted in another extreme that is liberal democracy, which is not bound by any set of Divine moral principles. The Islamic political system is again away from both extremes.

The term theocracy is translated as 'Rule of God', but in practice this system spiraled into a dictatorship of a group of religious elite. In Christian Theocracy the Pope was considered infallible, therefore his judgment was binding upon the people. This mindset is mentioned in the following verse of the Holy Quran and is equated with the grave sin of Shirk (associating partners with Allah).

"They have taken their rabbis and their monks as gods beside Allah, and also (they have taken) Christ the son of Mary (as god). And they were not commanded but to worship only One God. There is no god but He. Pure is He from what they associate with Him." (Surah At-Tauba, Chapter 9, Ayat 31)

As reported by Tirmizi on the authority of Adi bin Hatim (RAA) who was a Christian before accepting Islam, heard the Messenger of Allah (S.A.W.W) recite the above Ayat. He objected, "They do not worship their priests." The Prophet (S.A.W.W) explained, "Whatever their priests and rabbis call permissible, they accept as permissible; whatever they declare as forbidden, they consider as forbidden, and thus they worship them." (Reported in Tirmizi)

The Islamic political system is not a system of theocracy. The founder of Pakistan, Quaid-i-Azam Muhammad Ali Jinnah, once said:

"The great majority of us are Muslims. We follow the teachings of the Prophet Muhammed (S.A.W.W). We are members of the brotherhood of Islam in which all are equal in rights, dignity and self-respect. Consequently, we have a special and a very deep sense of unity. But make no mistake: Pakistan is not a theocracy or anything like it." [12]

Recovering from the ill experiences of theocratic models, Europe shifted towards another extreme, that is, the extreme of liberal democracy.

In this system the people collectively determine what is right and what is wrong, and they are not bound by any Divine moral system. The result is that parliaments are legalizing immoral, and unnatural practices like homosexuality. Incest may be the next. There is nothing to stop this immorality. A majority vote has the power to legalize anything. Such practices cannot be legalized in the Islamic system of democracy (Khilafah) even by a 100% vote.

The political system of Islam is based on the concept of Divine sovereignty and human vicegerency (Khilafah). In the Islamic system, people cannot make changes in matters which they find direct instructions given in the Holy Quran and Sunnah (life and teachings of Prophet Muhammad S.A.W.W).

For example, we know that drinking wine is Haram, that is, it is not allowed in Islam. Muslims cannot make it Halal (lawful) even by a 100% vote in its favour. On the other hand, in numerous other matters where there is no direct guidance found in the Holy Quran and Sunnah, decisions are reached by mutual consultation in a democratic manner.

While mentioning some of the qualities of righteous people, the Holy Quran says, "And those who answer the call of their Lord and establish worship, and whose affairs are a matter of counsel, and who spend of what We have bestowed on them." (Surah Ash-Shura, Chapter 42, Ayat 38) Some practical examples of areas of mutual consultation may be 'how many working hours', 'how many provinces', 'which city is to be the capital', 'making a war strategy', 'which language should be the national language', 'which technology to adopt', etc. Islam promotes mutual consultation in the decision-making process of such matters.

The aforementioned examples illustrating the balanced positions of Islam in the spiritual and socio-politico-economic realms prove that Islam is not an extremist system. The moderation in Islamic teachings is the most significant distinctive feature that truly sets the Islamic way apart from the methods followed by other creeds, civilizations, and philosophies. Even the specific details pertaining to the Islamic civilization are, indeed, stamped by a beautiful balance and moderation.

ISLAM, SCIENCE AND MODERNIZATION

Some of those without a proper study of Islam think that following the religion means adopting an outdated system of the stone ages. The fallacy of this gross misunderstanding can be appreciated through the succeeding discussion.

Islam is not opposed to science or scientific progress. Historically speaking, we find great Muslim scientists who, in their respective eras, carried scientific knowledge to newer heights, providing a strong base for the current scientific developments of the West.

American historian, journalist, racial anthropologist, eugenicist, and political theorist, Dr. Lothrop Stoddard writes, "For the first three centuries of its existence (Circa 650 A.C. - 1000 A.C.) the realm of Islam was the most civilized and progressive portion of the world. Studded with splendid cities, gracious mosques and quiet universities where the wisdom of the ancient world was preserved and appreciated, the Moslem world offered a striking contrast to the Christian West, then sunk in the night of the Dark Ages." [13]

Science has brought about many wonderful changes in the modern world. One must recall it was Islam that promoted science at a time when scientific progress had become stagnant throughout the world. Dr. Maurice Bucaille, who was a French medical doctor, member of the French Society of Egyptology, and an author, explains this relationship between Islam and science in his famous book 'The Bible, the Quran and Science':

"It is an established fact that at the time of the Quranic revelation i.e. within the period of roughly twenty years straddling hegira (622 A.D), scientific knowledge had not progressed for centuries and the period of activity in Islamic civilization, with its accompanying scientific upsurge, came after the close of the Quranic revelation."

He also writes, "Why should we be surprised at this when we know that, for Islam, religion and science have always been considered twin sisters? From the very beginning, Islam directed people to cultivate science; the application of this precept brought with it the prodigious strides in science taken during the great era of Islamic civilization, from which, before the Renaissance, the West itself benefited."

Regarding the Holy Quran, Dr. Maurice Bucaille writes, "…it is unconceivable for a human being (Muhammad PBUH) living in the seventh century A.D to have made statements in the Quran on a great variety of subjects that do not belong to his period and for them to be in keeping with what was to be known only centuries later. For me, there can be no human explanation to the Quran." [14] Please note that Dr. Maurice Bucaille converted to Islam after observing this miracle of the Holy Quran.

The renowned British orientalist Marmaduke Pickthall who later converted to Islam said in his book 'Islamic Culture': "The Quran undoubtedly gave a great impetus to learning especially in the field of natural sciences… The Muslims set out on their search for learning in the name of God at a time when Christians were destroying all the learning of the ancients in the name of Christ. They had destroyed the Library of Alexandria, they had murdered many philosophers, including the beautiful Hypatia. Learning was for them a devil's snare beloved of the pagans. They had no injunction to 'seek knowledge even though it was in China.' The manuscripts of Greek and Roman learning were publicly burnt by the priests… It was from the teaching of the Spanish Muslim Universities that Columbus got his notion that the world was round, though he too was forced under persecution to recant it all afterwards."

"When we remember that the Spanish Muslim Universities in the time of Khalifa Abdul Rahman III and the Eastern Muslim Universities in the time of Al-Mamun – I mention those two monarchs because it is specially recorded of their times – welcomed Christian and Jewish students on equality with the Muslims; and not only that, but entertained them at the Government expenses, and that hundreds of Christian students from the South of Europe and the countries of the East took advantage of the chance to escape from the ecclessiastical (Church – ed) leading strings; we can easily perceive what debt of gratitude modern European progress owes to Islam, while it owes nothing whatsoever to the Christian Church which persecuted, tortured and even burnt the learned." [15]

According to a BBC report, "From about 700 to 1700, many of history's finest scientists and technologists were to be found in the Muslim world. In Christian Europe the light of scientific inquiry had largely been extinguished with the collapse of the Roman Empire."

"But it survived, and indeed blazed brightly, elsewhere. From Moorish Spain across North Africa to Damascus, Baghdad, Persia and all the way to India, scientists in the Muslim world were at the forefront of developments in medicine, astronomy, engineering, hydraulics, mathematics, chemistry, map-making and exploration. A new touring exhibition, hosted by the Science Museum in London, celebrates their achievements." [16]

Marquis of Dufferin also acknowledged this fact in speeches delivered in India: "It is to Mussulman (Muslim) science, to Mussulman art, to Mussulman literature that Europe has been in a great measure indebted for its extrication from the darkness of the Middle ages." [17]

The preceding statements make it very clear that Islam is not at odds with science, rather it promotes scientific development. Islam also encourages modernization and continuous improvements. As one example, the modern numerals, called Arabic numerals, widely used today were most probably developed in India, but it was the Arabs who transmitted this system to the West. An Indian scholar arrived in Baghdad in 771, bringing with him a paper on astronomy that used the Indian numerical system, which drew the admiration of the Arabs because it was more economical than the Roman system. In time, the Arabs added a further improvement: the 'sifr' i.e zero.

'Modernity', by itself, is a praiseworthy desire and a natural urge of the human race. Were it not for this urge, man would not have reached the space exploration era from the stone-age and could not have gained access to airplanes and space crafts. Being a natural religion, Islam is not opposed to modernism as far as what is implied by the basic sense of the word. 'Modernity' is, however, a double-edged sword that can be used for the benefit of humanity or to cut its own throat. The challenge for Muslims today is to recognize these parameters of 'Modernity' in light of the guidance of Islam and to pursue advancement without overstepping the limits of the unalterable injunctions of Islam.

This can be appreciated through considering the case of the Industrial Revolution. The gamut of modern changes spurred by the Industrial Revolution can be grouped into two types. The first of these are desirable changes that were inevitable for advancement, without which it was not possible for science and technology to have attained their present standards.

It was due to these that mankind was benefited by the latest inventions, large-scale production facilities came into being, bridges and dams were constructed and a plethora of useful additions to human knowledge were made. This aspect of the Industrial Revolution was indeed praiseworthy, serving as a crucial stepping stone for the world to progress, and this is encouraged in Islam.

On the other hand, other societal changes grew rampant such as nudity, free sex, and usury, which bore no connection to scientific and industrial development. It has in fact been proven that they have served as an obstacle rather than support towards progress. These were unnecessarily affixed to the Industrial Revolution, and now realizing this error, many are sighing with grief. This is what (the evil) Islam calls against.

Thus, Islam is not against progress and modernity, in fact these are supported by Islam. Practicing Muslims cultivated science during the major part of their nearly 1400 year long history. Unfortunately, with their gradual religious and political decline, Muslims were also left behind in the field of science.

Chapter 6

ISLAM AND NON-MUSLIMS

"God does not forbid you from being good to those who have not fought you in the religion or driven you from your homes, or from being just towards them. God loves those who are just."

***(Al-Quran**, Surat al-Mumtahina, Chapter 60, Ayat 8)*

"In the name of God, the Merciful, the Compassionate. This is the assurance of safety which the servant of God, Umer, the Commander of the Faithful, has given to the people of Jerusalem. He has given them an assurance of safety for themselves for their property, their churches, their crosses, the sick and healthy of the city and for all the rituals which belong to their religion. Their churches will not be inhabited by Muslims and will not be destroyed. Neither they, nor the land on which they stand, nor their cross, nor their property will be damaged. They will not be forcibly converted…. Those who wish may go with the Byzantines and those who wish may return to their families. Nothing is to be taken from them before their harvest is reaped." [1]

These are the historical words that were delivered to the local Christian community after the peaceful takeover of Jerusalem in 637 AD by Caliph Umer (R.A.A), the most powerful person on earth at the time.

Hazrat Umer (R.A.A) was a senior companion of Prophet Muhammad (S.A.W.W) who succeeded Hazrat Abu Bakr (R.A.A) as the second caliph of the Rashidun Caliphate on August 23, 634. He was also an expert Muslim jurist known for his pious and just nature which earned him the epithet Al-Farooq, the one who distinguishes (between right and wrong)".

Michael Hart has included Caliph Umer (RAA) in his famous book 'The 100' in which he has discussed the 100 most influential personalities in the history of mankind. In the chapter about Caliph Umer (R.A.A) he writes:

"It may occasion some surprise that 'Umar' – a figure virtually unknown to the West – has been ranked higher than such famous men as Charlemagne and Julius Caesar. However, the conquests made by the Arabs under 'Umar', taking into account both their size and their duration, are substantially more important than those of either Caesar or Charlemagne." [2]

Alexander, who is considered to be the greatest conqueror of the world, conquered an area of 1.7 million square miles, whereas the area that came under the Islamic empire during Hazrat Umer's (R.A.A) rule was 2.2 million square miles. I have refrained from using the term 'conqueror' to refer to him as he was utterly unlike the normal association of the term with one driven by material motives. The Muslims honor him for being a great companion of Prophet Muhammad (S.A.W.W) and a great jurist of Islam.

His words quoted above provide the reader an instructive glimpse into the teachings of Islam regarding the treatment of non-Muslims.

RIGHTS OF NON-MUSLIMS

The unparalleled times of Hazrat Umer (R.A.A) and other pious companions of Prophet Muhammad (S.A.W.W) like Hazrat Abu Bakr (R.A.A), Hazrat Usman (R.A.A), and Hazrat Ali (R.A.A), are long over. That level of piety is not found in present-day Muslims.

But do Muslims still believe in the fair and kind treatment of non-Muslims?

The answer is a resounding yes.

On January 24, 1951, a group of 31 Ulema (Islamic scholars) of various schools of thought united upon a 22-point agenda for an Islamic state at a conference in Karachi, Pakistan. The group headed by Syed Suleman Nadavi included eminent Islamic scholars of the time like Maulana Maududi, Mufti Mohammad Shafi, Maulana Abdul Hamid Badayuni, Mufti Jafar Hussain, and Maulana Daud Ghaznavi. I am quoting the 4 points (out of the 22) that are either directly or indirectly related to the treatment of non-Muslims by the Muslim state:

Point # 6: The State will provide basic necessities to people like food, clothing, housing, medical treatment, and education, <u>irrespective of their religion or race</u> for those who are not able to earn their living or are temporarily unemployed.

Point # 7: All citizens of the State will enjoy the rights given to them by Islam. For example, the right of security of life, wealth & honor; <u>freedom for religion or sect</u>; freedom for worship; individual freedom; freedom of expression; freedom for movement; freedom for collective meetings; freedom to earn; equal opportunities of advancement; freedom to take benefit from welfare organizations.

Point # 10: <u>Non-Muslim citizens will be free to follow their religion</u>, worship, culture, and religious education within the framework of the State law. In their private matters they have the right to seek decisions according to their religious law or cultural practices.

Point # 11: <u>All agreements with non-Muslim citizens</u> will be honored within the framework of Islamic law.

These points make clear that the present-day mainstream Muslims recognize the importance and religious merit of the good treatment of non-Muslims.

Islam does not believe in selective morality, therefore in Islam, Muslims are commanded to be just and fair not only towards Muslims but also towards non-Muslims. It is clearly stated in the Holy Quran, "O you who believe, be steadfast for (obeying the commands of) Allah, (and) witnesses for justice. Malice against a people should not prompt you to avoid doing justice. Do justice. That is nearer to Taqwa. Fear Allah. Surely, Allah is All-Aware of what you do." (Surah Al-Maidah, Chapter 5, Ayat 8)

Forced conversion to Islam:

Agenda point # 10 and the historical evidence provided in the form of Hazrat Umer's (R.A.A) words for the non-Muslims of Jerusalem, also demonstrates that the forceful conversion of non-Muslims is not allowed in Islam.

Although vast lands were conquered by the early Muslims all throughout the globe, citizens of those conquered lands were not coerced into accepting Islam. Rather, the non-Muslim citizens of conquered lands were protected by the Muslims. This behavior was in line with the following instruction of the Holy Quran:

"Let there be no compulsion in religion…" (Surah Al-Baqarah, Chapter 2, Ayat 256)

Many of those belonging to the extensive lands conquered by the Muslim armies accepted Islam, not by force, but by the appeal of the great new religion. It was pure faith in One God, emphasis upon His Mercy and good treatment by Muslims that drew huge numbers into the fold of Islam. Others continued to remain Jews, Christians, etc., and to this day communities of the followers of other faiths are found in Muslim lands.

The spread of Islam was not limited to its miraculous early expansion outside of Arabia. In later years, the Turks embraced Islam peacefully as did a great fraction of the people of the Indian subcontinent and the Malay-speaking world. In Africa as well, Islam further spread during the past centuries even under the gripping power and control of European colonial rulers. Today, Islam continues to grow including in Europe and the USA where Muslims now comprise a significant minority.

Noted historian De Lacy O'Leary writes in the book 'Islam at the cross road', "History makes it clear however, that the legend of fanatical Muslims sweeping through the world and forcing Islam at the point of the sword upon conquered races is one of the most fantastically absurd myth that historians have ever repeated." [3]

Dhimmi (or Zimmi):

A non-Muslim living in a Muslim state is called a 'dhimmi'. It is a historical term referring to non-Muslims living in an Islamic state with legal protection. The term 'dhimmi' literally means "protected person". Ms. Tesneem Alkiek, a Muslim scholar, provides a worthy, comprehensive explanation of the term in her research paper 'Religious Minorities under Muslim rule':

"Religious minorities are known as dhimmīs, short for ahl al-dhimmah, or people of the dhimmah, a term that later became synonymous with the People of the Book. The original meaning of al-dhimmah, however, meant protection, and it was often short for dhimmat–Allah wa-rasūlih, or the "protection of God and His Prophet." In short, the concept originally had a divine connotation, or a meaning that was directly related to the power of God. However, the concept soon morphed into a technical legal term with the progression of classical scholarship, and it consequently lost its transcendent dimension. As a result, ahl al-dhimmah, or people of the dhimmah, has become a legal term and not a reference to the recipients of divine protection. It is important to discuss the etymology of the word because it demonstrates the significance of the people of the dhimmah who, at the very root of it all, are people who were to be protected on behalf of God and His Prophet – an immense responsibility. This status is awarded to People of the Book (who according to many scholars includes Zoroastrians and others) who agree through contract to pay the jizyah, or poll-tax, in exchange for that protection. In sum, the formation of the people of the dhimmah was rooted in religious minorities paying a tax that exempted them from military service." [4]

Jizya tax:

Jizyah is the tax paid by non-Muslims living in a Muslim State. Khiraj tax is also levied on non-Muslims on their lands. Some people may think that levying Jizya and Khiraj taxes on only non-Muslim citizens of the state is unfair. I used to feel the same way before my detailed study of Islam and my study of modern economics during my MBA.

Taxes are levied by all modern states irrespective of religion. The more a country believes in public welfare, the more its citizens have to pay in taxes to support state welfare activities, unless a state is affluent due to other reasons like the possession of massive oil reserves and gold resources.

An Islamic system is also a welfare system, and it therefore needs funds to support its many welfare activities for both Muslims and non-Muslims. Funds are also required for conducting routine state activities.

These are collected from non-Muslims in the form of Jizya or Khiraj taxes, whereas Muslims pay Zakat and Usher (on lands) along with other payments. As Zakat and Usher are not normally referred to as tax but are considered a religious obligation as the prayer, these cannot be levied on non-Muslims who instead pay the taxes just mentioned. In return, non-Muslims are exempted from compulsory military service in the case of foreign aggression and are entitled to guaranteed security and protection. If the Muslim State cannot protect those who paid Jizya, then the amount they paid is restored to them. Please note that according to Islamic jurisprudence, Jizya tax is not levied upon women, children, the disabled, blind, self-secluded priests, and beggars with no source of earning.

During the early days of Islam, the people of Hairah contributed the sum agreed upon. They clearly mentioned that they paid this Jizya on the condition that, "The Muslims and their leader protect us from those who would oppress us, whether they be Muslims or others." In his agreement with the people of certain cities near Al-Haira, Hazrat Khalid bin Walid (R.A.A) recorded, "If we are able to protect you, we deserve the collection of Jizya."

In return for the payment of Jizya tax, the Muslim state not only provides a guarantee for the protection of the life and wealth of non-Muslims, but also financial support to their poor. And, as stated, in the case of any external attack on the country, the Caliph, who can order Muslims to participate in the war, cannot order non-Muslims to similarly partake in the war effort. Moreover, in such a case non-Muslims must be provided full protection against external aggressors.

In the post-colonial era, I do not think any Muslim country has levied Jizya or Khiraj tax on non-Muslims. All citizens of the state pay taxes irrespective of their religion. Practicing Muslims pay additional amounts to the poor in the form of Zakat, Usher, and many other obligatory religious payments. Thus, a practicing Muslim effectively pays much heavier amounts.

FURTHER HISTORICAL EVIDENCES

The following are some lived examples from history illustrating the noble and just treatment of non-Muslims by the Muslims:

Once Caliph Umer (R.A.A) saw a beggar in the streets of Madina. The Caliph went to him and asked, "Why are you begging? Are you not receiving maintenance (allowance) from Bait-ul-Maal". The beggar replied; "I am a Jew and I am doing this so that I can pay the Jizya (tax)". Caliph Umer (R.A.A) took him by his hand to the Bait-ul-Maal (a financial institution responsible for the administration of taxes in Islamic states) and decreed, "In the name of Allah you pay Jizya all your life and then you get betrayed when you reach old age." Caliph Umer (R.A.A) ordered to provide that man pension and from that day it was so ordered for all Jews, Christians, and others.

After taking over the control of Jerusalem from the Christians, Caliph Umer (R.A.A) visited the holy places in Jerusalem in the company of the Patriarch of the city. When the time of prayer came, the Patriarch invited the Caliph to offer his prayers in the Church of the Resurrection. Hazrat Umer (R.A.A) declined, saying that if he were to do that later Muslims might wrongfully claim the Church as their own place of worship.

Caliph Usman (R.A.A) was a companion ofProphet Muhammad (S.A.W.W) who succeeded Hazrat Umer (R.A.A) as the third caliph of the Rashidun Caliphate. His instructions given to the military officers were, "You are to protect the life and property of both Muslims and non-Muslims. The laws made hitherto under Umer (R.A.A) were made as a result of consultations, therefore do not breach them."

Caliph Ali (R.A.A) was a companion of Prophet Muhammad (S.A.W.W) who succeeded Hazrat Usman (R.A.A) as the fourth caliph of the Rashidun Caliphate. Once Caliph Ali's (R.A.A) armor was lost. He saw it with a Jew who was trying to sell it. Caliph Ali (R.A.A) asked him for his armor. The Jew refused to give it back and asserted that the armor belongs to him. The case was therefore taken to the court of justice where Qazi Sharih was the judge. Qazi Sharih asked Caliph Ali (R.A.A) for witnesses to prove his ownership. Caliph Ali (R.A.A) forwarded Mr. Qanbur along with his son. Qazi Sharih said that a son's witness in favor of his father is not acceptable by the court. The judge announced his verdict in favour of the Jew and against the Caliph.

A city in modern day Syria was under the rule of the Muslims where many Jews and Christians were living. A companion of Prophet Muhammad (S.A.W.W), Hazrat Abu Ubaidah bin Jarrah (R.A.A), was their ruler.

One day the Muslims received the news that the Roman emperor Heraclius has sent a big army to attack the city. There were not enough Muslims in the city to defend it, and the Muslim armies from other areas would likely have taken much time to reach for backup. Hazrat Abu Ubaidah (R.A.A), after consultation with other Muslims, decided that they should transfer to some safer place and wait for backup. The Jizya collected previously from the non-Muslim local population was therefore returned and it was announced, "We are unable to help and defend you therefore now the matter is in your hand." This also meant that the non-Muslims could open the gates of the city for the Roman emperor Heraclius. It was additionally announced, "We have returned your money because we do not like that despite taking money from you we are unable to defend your land. We are going to another place and are sending message to our brothers for help. We will then fight our enemy. If Allah gives us victory, then we will fulfill our covenant with you unless you yourself do not like so." The non-Muslim population replied, "We indeed love your government and your justice, as compared to the cruelty and coercion in which we were living before you."

The Sultan of Morocco Muhammad ibn Abdullah, issued an edict on February 5, 1864 CE: "To our civil servants and agents who perform their duties as authorized representatives in our territories, we issue the following edict: 'They must deal with the Jewish residents of our territories according to the absolute standard of justice established by God. The Jews must be dealt with by the law on an equal basis with others so that none suffers the least injustice, oppression, or abuse. Nobody from their own community or outside shall be permitted to commit any offense against them or their property. Their artisans and craftsmen may not be scripted into service against their will, and must be paid full wages for serving the state. Any oppression will cause the oppressor to be in darkness on Judgment Day and we will not approve of any such wrongdoing."

"Everyone is equal in the sight of our law, and we will punish anyone who wrongs or commits aggression against the Jews with divine aid. This order which we have stated here is the same law that has always been known, established, and stated. We have issued this edict simply to affirm and warn anyone who may wish to wrong them, so the Jews may have a greater sense of security and those intending harm may be deterred by greater sense of fear." [5]

The reign of the Seljuk Turks was also marked by the just and compassionate outlook of Islam. In his book 'The Preaching of Islam', Thomas Arnold explains the Christians' willingness to come under Seljuk rule: "This same sense of security of religious life under Muslim rule led many of the Christians of Asia Minor, also, about the same time, to welcome the advent of the Saljuq Turks as their deliverers… In the reign of Michael VIII (1261-1282), the Turks were often invited to take possession of the smaller towns in the interior of Asia Minor by the inhabitants, that they might escape from the tyranny of the empire; and both rich and poor often emigrated into Turkish dominions."

Similarly, non-Muslims were granted many rights in the pre-Ottoman Islamic states. Georgetown University's Professor of Religion and International Relations John L. Esposito describes how Jews and Christians who came under the administration of Muslim states met with enormous understanding: "For many non-Muslim populations in Byzantine and Persian territories already subjugated to foreign rulers, Islamic rule meant an exchange of rulers, the new ones often more flexible and tolerant, rather than a loss of independence. Many of these populations now enjoyed greater local autonomy and often paid lower taxes... Islam proved a more tolerant religion, providing greater religious freedom for Jews and indigenous Christians."

Sultan Saladin Ayubi entered Jerusalem in 1187 and freed it from 88 years of Crusader occupation. When the Crusaders had taken the city 88 years earlier, they had killed all the Muslims inside it, and for that reason they feared that Saladin would do the same to them. However, he did not touch even one Christian in the city. Furthermore, he merely ordered the Latin (Catholic) Christians to leave, while the Orthodox Christians, who were not Crusaders, were allowed to live in the city and worship as they chose. In the words of John L. Esposito:

"The Muslim army was as magnanimous in victory as it had been tenacious in battle. Civilians were spared; churches and shrines were generally left untouched... Saladin was faithful to his word and compassionate toward noncombatants."

Karen Armstrong describes the second capture of Jerusalem in these words:

"On 2 October 1187 Saladin and his army entered Jerusalem as conquerors and for the next 800 years Jerusalem would remain a Muslim city. Saladin kept his word, and conquered the city according to the highest Islamic ideals. He did not take revenge for the 1099 massacre, as the Qur'an advised (16:127), and now that hostilities had ceased he ended the killing (2:193-194). Not a single Christian was killed and there was no plunder.

The ransoms were deliberately very low... Saladin... released many of them freely, as the Qur'an urged.... His brother al-Adil was so distressed by the plight of the prisoners that he asked Saladin for a thousand of them for his own use and then released them on the spot... All the Muslim leaders were scandalised to see the rich Christians escaping with their wealth, which could have been used to ransom all the prisoners... [The Patriarch] Heraclius paid his ten-dinar ransom like everybody else and was even provided with a special escort to keep his treasure safe during the journey to Tyre."

It was not only the Christians but also the Jews that attained peace and security with the conquest of Jerusalem by the Muslims. In one of his works, the well-known Spanish-Jewish poet Yehuda al-Harizi expressed his thoughts as follows:

"God ...decided that the sanctuary would no longer rest in the hands of the sons of Esau... Thus in the year 4950 of Creation [AD 1190] God aroused the spirit of the prince of the Ishmaelites [Salah al-Din], a prudent and courageous man, who came with his entire army, besieged Jerusalem, took it and had it proclaimed throughout the country that he would receive and accept the race of Ephraim, wherever they came from. And so we came from all corners of the world to take up residence here. We now live in the shadow of peace."

CONTEMPORARY INSTANCES

The few misguided occurrences of terror are not representative of the great majority of Muslims residing peacefully as contributing citizens of Western societies. There are many instances of Muslims having risen to the occasion to be of vital assistance in adverse times. For example:

A fire broke out in a 24-story apartment building in the UK in June 2017 in which many people died. Many more would have been killed in the incident if young Muslim men had not come to their rescue.

Reporting this tragic event and the rescue efforts provided by Muslim boys, a UK newspaper wrote: "Muslim boys up late for Ramadan 'saved lives' by knocking on people's doors when fire broke out during Grenfell Tower blaze. …Muslims who were up late observing Ramadan were among heroes who saved lives in the Grenfell Tower fire. … A woman filmed near the scene told reporters: 'If it wasn't for all these young Muslim boys around here helping us coming from the mosque a lot more people would have been dead.' 'They were the first people with bags of water giving to people and helping, running and telling people.' A local woman told HuffPost UK: 'Muslim boys saved people's lives. They ran around knocking on people's doors. Thank God for Ramadan'. [6]

In the USA, on the night of October 1, 2017, a gunman opened fire on a crowd of concertgoers at the Route 91 Harvest music festival on the Las Vegas Strip in Nevada. As a result 58 people were killed and 546 injured by the gunman, 64-year-old Stephen Paddock, from Mesquite, Nevada. The incident was the deadliest mass shooting committed by an individual in the United States. In order to help the victims' families, an Islamic organization ran a fundraising campaign. The campaign page stated, "In what has been called the deadliest mass shooting in modern United States history, the shooting at the Route 91 Harvest Festival in Las Vegas, Nevada left 58 people dead and more than 500 injured. Families from across the country, and even outside of it, have lost their loved ones in this senseless and devastating act of violence. This is why a collective of American Muslim leaders and groups have united, in this campaign run by CelebrateMercy, to raise funds for the victims' families."

"…Although this campaign is organized by Muslims, we welcome people of all faiths to contribute (all donations are tax-deductible). No amount of money will bring back the victims, but we do hope to lessen their family's burdens in some way. Let's all stand together against the tragic killing of innocent lives." [7]

According to a January 27, 2017, TIME magazine report: "Even in the darkest times, there are heroes—though sometimes they may be the people we least expect. That's the message a global nonprofit group hopes to spread Friday on Holocaust Remembrance Day, when it displays a small exhibit in a New York synagogue highlighting the little-known stories of Muslims who risked their lives to rescue Jewish people from persecution during World War II."

"Though the two religious groups are often presented in opposition, this exhibit is a reminder that they have also shared an important history of cooperation and mutual assistance.

The tales include those of Khaled Abdul Wahab, who sheltered about two dozen Jews in Tunisia, and Abdol Hossein Sardari, an Iranian diplomat who is credited with helping thousands of Jews escape Nazi soldiers by issuing them passports.

The group also recognizes the Pilkus, a Muslim family in Albania who harbored young Johanna Neumann and her mother in their home during the German occupation and convinced others that the two were family members visiting from Germany. 'They put their lives on the line to save us,' Neumann, now 86, told TIME on Friday. 'If it had come out that we were Jews, the whole family would have been killed.'

'What these people did, many European nations didn't do,' she added. 'They all stuck together and were determined to save Jews.'

The collection of 15 stories shows how people organically came to protect one another, even in extreme environments of war and conflict, organizers said." [8]

IS ISLAM ANTI-SEMATIC

Some people think that Islam is an anti-sematic religion. This impression is, however, untrue.

Numerous examples quoted in this chapter relate to the good treatment of Jews by Muslims, and history is replete with such examples. These provide clear proof that those who portray Islam as anti-sematic are grossly mistaken. Throughout the centuries Muslims have, in fact, protected and honored Jews.

Prophet Muhammad (S.A.W.W) along with many of his companions migrated to the city of Medina from Makkah and laid the foundation of the state of Medina. Prophet Muhammad (S.A.W.W) allowed the Jews to become a party to the Constitution of Medina signed with the Arab clans of the Aws and Khazraj, thus ensuring the survival of the Jews as a separate religious group among the Muslims.

The way the Jews settled in Muslim Ottoman lands during the time of Sultan Beyazid II, after being subjected to massacre and exile in the Catholic kingdoms of Spain and Portugal, is a fine example of the compassion that Islamic society brings with it. The Catholic kings, who ruled much of Spain at the time, brought grave pressure to bear on the Jews who had formerly lived in peace under Muslim rule in Andalusia. While Muslims, Christians, and Jews were able to live side by side in peace in Andalusia during the Muslim rule, the Catholic monarchs tried to force the whole country to become Christian, and declared war on the Muslims while oppressing the Jews. At last the last Muslim ruler in the Granada region in southern Spain was overthrown in 1492. Muslims were subjected to terrible slaughter, and those Jews who refused to change their religion were sent into exile. One group of these Jews, without a homeland, sought shelter in the Ottoman Empire. The Ottoman fleet, under the command of Kemal Reis, brought the exiled Jews, and those Muslims who had survived the slaughter to the land of the Ottomans.

During the Nazi occupation of France in World War II, the Grand Mosque of Paris saved the lives of many Jews. The grand mosque constructed in 1926 had space for a community center, library, restaurant, clinic, and apartments for the functionaries. It was built upon a labyrinth of subterranean tunnels and rooms, areas that had been excavated for building stones for the city of Paris. These underground passages and catacombs served as hiding places and escape routes for those hunted by the French police and Gestapo.

The rescue and escape of Jews was under the leadership of the Rector, Si Kaddour Benghabrit, a sophisticated Algerian born diplomat, who was considered the most powerful Muslim in France at the time. The clerics provided sanctuary, certificates of Muslim identity and safe passage for those who sought their help. [9]

Muslims are not against Jews; however, many Muslims are against the state of Israel, which they believe was unlawfully created by occupying Palestinian land. They are opposed to its hostile policies of aggression in the Arab world and the manner in which Israeli troops handle Palestinians. Nearly 700,000 Palestinians lost their homeland and became refugees with the creation of Israel and its subsequent wars with the Arab countries. This Palestinian refugee crisis remains unresolved as yet.

Even many religious Jews are against the state of Israel and the Zionist movement. According to a Jewish website, "They (Zionists) start wars that endanger the Jewish People, for the sake of their own political interests. …According to the Torah the path of safety is following ways of peace not starting fights with other nations, as the Zionists do. …The most important Rabbis and the majority of religious Jewry are opposed to Zionism, but their voice is not heard because of Zionist control of American news media." [10]

The Holy Quran has instructed the Muslims to treat non-Muslims courteously with a spirit of kindness and generosity, given they are not hostile towards Muslims. According to the Quran: "God does not forbid you from those who do not fight you because of religion and do not expel you from your homes – from dealing kindly and justly with them. Indeed, God loves those who act justly. God only forbids you from those who fight you because of religion and expel you from your homes and aid in your expulsion – (forbids) that you make allies of them. And whoever makes allies of them, then it is those who are the wrongdoers." (Al-Quran, Chapter 60, Surat al-Mumtahina, Ayat 8 & 9)

Divine commandments to treat non-Muslims in this manner are taken very seriously by Muslims. These are not just verses to be recited, but Divine Will to be acted upon.

There may be examples of the mistreatment of non-Muslims by the Muslims, including targeted terror acts in the recent past. Such wrongful treatment is, however, entirely against the teachings of Islam, and it is therefore always condemned by the mainstream Muslim majority.

Chapter 7

THE CONCEPT OF JIHAD

"Simply talking about Jihad does not mean a terrorist organization has been found."

(Udo Jacob, Nigerian Intellectual & Academician) [1]

The term 'Jihad' rings a different bell for different people. Many people understand it only to mean to Muslims waging holy war, whereas others contend that the term has a wider meaning, limiting which to a military sense is unjustified. Among Muslims, although the term Jihad is commonly used to refer to Holy war, it carries a larger meaning of struggle in the way of God which includes other forms of Jihad that do not involve physical combat. Generally, when used without any qualifier, the term Jihad is understood in its military purport.

It is wrong to equate or intermingle the concepts of Jihad and terrorism. However frequent use of the term Jihad by terrorists has created an impression in many minds that Jihad is the Islamic name given to the undertaking of violence (whether in form of conventional war or acts of terrorism) by Muslims against non-Muslims. This has stirred much confusion and falsity about the Islamic concept of Jihad. And this is the reason for the inclusion of this chapter in this book, in order to clarify the misunderstandings surrounding the term.

MEANING OF JIHAD

'Jihad' is an Arabic word which means "to struggle or strive, to exert oneself" for a praiseworthy aim. In the context of Islam, it can refer to any kind of striving in the way of God which involves either spiritual or personal effort. This is the essence of Jihad in Islam. It can take many forms depending on the circumstances.

Suppose there is a situation in which it becomes extremely difficult or even dangerous for a person to profess Islam and remain true to its teachings. In such a circumstance, Jihad would mean doing the best for oneself, to stay firmly devoted to Islam.

Should Muslims start drifting away from Islam through their own folly or negligence, then, at such a time, to devote one's time and energy to their religious revival and reform would too be a type of Jihad. Similarly, striving against one's own sinful and lustful desires is also a form of Jihad. To speak a just word before a tyrannical ruler (whether Muslim or non-Muslim) is again a form of Jihad.

Should believers in Allah s.w.t and the Prophet Muhammad (S.A.W.W) be in power and the conditions demand that collective force be used for the defense and assistance of faith, then the use of force for the defense and assistance of faith according to the rules laid down for it in Islam will constitute Jihad. Therefore, the word Jihad is also used to refer to a war waged by the Muslims for the defense or advancement of Islam, its interests, and ideals.

CLASSIFICATIONS OF JIHAD

Jihad can be of various types depending upon the type of struggle we are talking about. There are a number of ways of classifying Jihad as discussed by various Muslim scholars.

Some Muslim authorities distinguish between the 'greater jihad' (Jihad-i-Akbar), which pertains to spiritual self-perfection, and the 'lesser jihad' (Jihad-i-Asghar), defined as warfare.

Ibn Rushd (14 April 1126 – 10 December 1198), often Latinized as Averroes, was a medieval Muslim polymath. Ibn Rushd divides Jihad into the following four kinds:

1. 'Jihad by the heart', that is one's struggle to keep away from bad thoughts and to keep one's mind clean.

2. 'Jihad by the tongue', that is to speak up against the evils present in a society.

3. 'Jihad by the hand', that is using one's hands or exerting physical effort to stop an evil.

4. 'Jihad by the sword', that is armed conflict against evil.

Ibn Rushd defines 'Jihad by the tongue' as to commend good conduct and forbid the wrong. [2]

Dr. M. Amir Ali, a Muslim scholar in his article 'Islam, Jihad and Terrorism' [3] mentions the following three levels of Jihad:

Inner Jihad:

A personal struggle within one's self to submit to Allah, fight evil within one's self, achieve higher moral and educational standards.

Social Jihad:

Jihad against evil, injustice, and oppression within one's self, family, and society.

Physical Jihad or an armed struggle:

Jihad against all that prevents Muslims from servitude to God (Allah), people from knowing Islam, defense of a Muslim society (country), retribution against tyranny, and/or when a Muslim is removed from their homeland by force.

Dr. Israr Ahmed (26 April 1932 – 14 April 2010) was a globally renowned Islamic scholar and philosopher from Pakistan. In his book 'Jihad-fi-sabi-Lillah' [4], he provides a comprehensive breakdown of Jihad into several groups and subgroups which covers almost all the categories discussed by other scholars. His classification is as follows:

Jihad-fi-sabil-i-hayat (Struggle for existence):

Every living thing struggles for its existence in this world. This is also true for human beings. In order to survive, one has to provide oneself, and in many cases one's family, with food, shelter, and other necessities of life.

When a pious Muslim engages in this struggle for his or her survival in this competitive world then it is also a kind of Jihad and a praiseworthy deed. This type of Jihad is called 'Jihad-fi-sabil-i-hayat' that is 'struggle for existence'.

Jihad-fi-sabil-i-huqooq (Struggle for rights):

Many times human beings must also strive hard to obtain their rights. When a pious Muslim struggles for this cause, then it is also a kind of Jihad. This type of Jihad is called 'Jihad-fi-sabil-i-huqooq' that is 'struggle for rights'.

One basic human right is the right to freedom. It is not uncommon for nations to have to struggle against foreign occupying forces to secure their right of freedom. Such struggle for freedom by Muslims is also a kind of Jihad and is known as 'Jihad-fi-sabil-i-hurriat' that is 'struggle for freedom'.

Jihad-fi-sabi-Lillah (Struggle in the way of God):

People are often deeply influenced by a certain ideology or way of life. For instance, people may be very convinced of the Communist, or on the other hand, Capitalist ideology. Supporters of these ideologies may struggle to promote them and to establish systems on their basis. To cite an example, stalwarts of the communist ideology offered by Karl Marx (5 May 1818 – 14 March 1883) of Germany, were ultimately successful in bringing about the Bolshevik revolution in Russia in 1917. In a similar manner advocates of the Capitalist ideology strive to fortify and promote this ideology throughout the world. This has been to the extent that wars were even fought by the USA in Vietnam and Korea to protect the Capitalist ideology and counter the expansion of Communism. In the same way, if Muslims are promoting the Islamic ideology, then it is also a kind of Jihad known as 'Jihad-fi-sabi-Lillah', that is, struggle in the way of God. This struggle in the way of God consists of three stages:

<u>First stage</u>: In this stage a person strives to keep himself or herself away from all sorts of evil and strives to follow the teachings of Islam. This first stage of Jihad-fi-sabi-Lillah, comprises the following three components:

1. Struggle against one's own sinful and lustful desires.

2. Struggle against Satan and his its invisible companions who constantly incite us to sin. One has to keep oneself on the right path against all such incitements of Satan.

3. Struggle against evils in a society. One's surroundings may be full of sinful and immoral activities like injustice, exploitation, bribery, nudity, alcoholism, cruelty, racism, etc., all of which one must strive hard to keep away from.

<u>Second stage</u>: In the second stage, a person begins his or her struggle against the wrong beliefs and ideologies found in society. This struggle takes the form of inviting people towards the true path of Islam. It also involves enjoining the right and forbidding the wrong. As per the teachings of Islam, one has to act wisely in inviting people towards Islam.

According to the Holy Quran: "Invite (people) to the way of your Lord with wisdom and good counsel. And argue with them in the best of manners. Surely, your Lord knows best the one who deviates from His way, and He knows best the ones who are on the right path." (Surah Nahl, Chapter 16, Ayat 125)

<u>Third stage</u>: The third stage consists of the struggle for the establishment of the Islamic system at the state level. This can be called the struggle for an Islamic revolution in a country. This is not the work of an individual rather it requires a group of people or the formation of a party. This struggle can take three forms:

1. Passive resistance

2. Active resistance

3. Physical conflict.

The classification of Jihad by Dr. Israr Ahmed is quite exhaustive in which he has covered many areas like the conflict within a person, the propagation of one's ideology, Conflict, etc.

He has even differentiated Jihad-fi-sabi-Lillah (Struggle in the way of God) from other forms of Jihad like the struggle for existence or one's rights. While his classification does not seem to fully address the Jihad that consists of armed conflict between two nations, he has touched upon Jihad against foreign occupying forces under the heading of Jihad-fi-sabil-i-huqooq.

These examples all show that there are a number of ways in which Jihad can be classified. Most importantly, it is evident from these examples that Jihad can be both combative as well as non-combative.

COMBATIVE JIHAD

According to Sir Albert Einstein, "The world is a dangerous place, not because of those who do evil, but because of those who look on and do nothing." [5]

Many rightly claim that Islam is a religion of peace. But being a religion of peace does not mean that Islam altogether rules out the very possibility of war. Rather, the implication of Islam being a religion of peace is that Muslims are forbidden from committing cruelty, killing the innocent, and destroying life and property. Such unjustified violence has no place in Islam.

In certain circumstances, Islam allows Muslims to forcefully strive against perpetrators of cruelty and injustice. This can be likened to a doctor prescribing surgery on a patient to get rid of a tumor that cannot be treated through regular medication. In much the same way, the use of force sometimes becomes necessary to get rid of tumors of evil in the world that are otherwise incurable. This takes the form of combative Jihad.

There are many places in the Holy Quran and Ahadith of Prophet Muhammad (S.A.W.W) that talk about combative Jihad. This does not mean that combative jihad is the only issue addressed by the Quran and Ahadith as those who cherry pick Islamic quotations and reproduce them out of context would like to portray.

There is another term, 'Qital', that is used in the Holy Quran to refer to combative Jihad. The term 'Qital' comes from the word 'Qatal' which means to kill someone. 'Qital' means two-way killing, thus referring to a war in which the soldiers of the fighting armies are killed. One important point is that Qital is a kind of Jihad but not every Jihad is Qital. It is like saying that all women are human beings but not all human beings are women. Hence the term Jihad is also sometimes used in the Quran to refer to war.

Following are some verses of the Holy Quran that talk about combative Jihad. In each of these verses, the term Qital is used in the original Arabic text to refer to combat instead of the term Jihad:

"Permission (to fight) is given to those against whom fighting is launched, because they have been wronged, and Allah is powerful to give them victory. (They are) the ones who were expelled from their homes without any just reason, except that they say .Our Lord is Allah. Had Allah not been repelling some people by means of some others, the monasteries, the churches, the synagogues and the mosques where Allah's name is abundantly recited would have been demolished. Allah will definitely help those who help Him (by defending the religion prescribed by Him.) Surely Allah is Powerful, Mighty. (Surah Hajj, Chapter 22, Ayat 39 & 40)

"What has happened to you that you do not fight in the way of Allah, and for the oppressed among men, women and children who say, Our Lord, take us out from this town whose people are cruel, and make for us a supporter from Your own, and make for us a helper from Your own." (Surah Nisa, Chapter 4, Ayat 75)

"Would you not fight a people who broke their oaths and conspired to expel the Messenger, and it was they who started (fighting) against you for the first time? Do you fear them? But Allah has greater right that you fear Him, if you are believers." (Surah Tauba, Chapter 9, Ayat 13)

"Fight in the way of Allah against those who fight you, and do not transgress. Verily, Allah does not like the transgressors." (Surah Baqarah, Chapter 2, Ayat 190)

Combative Jihad can be of two types, 1) Defensive ('di-fa-ee'), and 2) Offensive ('iq-daa-mee').

The fight to defend one's life and property against criminals is an example of defensive Jihad. In the same way, countries have armed forces for the plausible need to defend itself against foreign aggression.

Enhancing the influence of righteousness, freeing people from tyrants, and reducing the political influence of an evil system, are some of the possible objectives of offensive Jihad. It is necessary to have state permission and guidance especially in the case of offensive Jihad. An individual or non-state actor cannot declare Jihad against a nation state. Secondly, the rules Islam has prescribed for Jihad must be scrupulously observed at the time of combative Jihad to minimize violence.

One thing that needs to be clarified here is that not all wars fought by Muslims can be called Jihad. For example, wars serving nationalistic goals or wars fought for purely material gain are not Jihad. A war fought by a Muslim army is Jihad when it is fought for a noble cause and for seeking the pleasure of Allah s.w.t Almighty.

MISINTERPRETATION OF JIHAD

Pakistan has long been facing the problem of terrorism. Pakistani armed forces have successfully carried out a military operation, 'Zarb-i-Azab', against terrorists within the country as a countermeasure. In addition to the military operation, terrorism is being fought on multiple other fronts including at the intellectual and religious levels.

In early 2018, a document titled 'Paigham-i-Pakistan' [6] was published in Pakistan denouncing all forms of terrorism in the country. This document was prepared in accordance with the injunctions of the Holy Qur'an, the Sunnah of the Prophet Muhammad (S.A.W.W), and the Constitution of Pakistan.

The document was originally developed by the Islamic Research Institute at International Islamic University, Islamabad and later improved and revised by eminent Islamic scholars of various schools of thought and professors of different national universities.

Assistance in the preparation of this document was also provided by distinguished religious scholars of Pakistan from Dar-ul-Uloom Karachi, Dar-ul-Uloom Muhammadiah Ghausia Bhera Sharif, Jamia Binoria Karachi, Jamiat al-Muntazar Lahore, Jamia Ashrafia Lahore, Jamia Haqqania Akora Khattak, Jamia Muhammadiah Islamabad and Jamia Faridiah Islamabad. 'Paigham-i-Pakistan' reflects the collective, unanimous stance of the State of Pakistan against terrorism and extremism. I am reproducing a few excerpts from the document below that relate to the topic of combative Jihad:

"Terrorists do not differentiate between Jihad and traditional wars. The concept of Jihad is monumental; which encompasses personal and social aspects of Muslim's life. This process continues throughout the life in various forms. One of which is qital, which under specific circumstances is the responsibility of the State. On the other hand, for traditional warfare the Holy Qur'an has used the term 'harb'."

"Life of the Holy Prophet (peace be upon him) teaches us that qital is an exception, whereas, peace and reconciliation shall prevail under normal circumstances.

Islamic Jurists are of the opinion that qital is not mandatory under normal situations. Rather, it is partially obligatory (Farz kifayah). Therefore, it is required that qital should only be declared by the State. The Treaty of Medina reflects the same example in which the authority and announcement of war was in the hands of Prophet Muhammad (peace be upon him).

According to Islamic jurists, no activity leading to war can be initiated without the consent of the state ruler or his appointed commanders. A soldier cannot attack the enemy in his personal capacity without the permission of his commander. Islamic jurists also say that war cannot be waged without the permission of the government and moreover, it cannot be started just to overcome the enemy.

It is right of the government to allow fighting or waging war which is further subject to the vulnerable security situation of the state.

The Holy Qur'an states: 'But if the enemy incline towards peace, do thou (also) incline towards peace, and trust in Allah: for He is One that heareth and knoweth (all things).' (Qur'an 8:61)

In light of the above-mentioned Qur'anic verse, Muslim jurists do not justify every type of war, they specifically warn against waging war only to gain power, as terrorists are doing nowadays, even though they bring farfetched religious arguments in support of their actions." [7]

Under the heading 'Trend of Taking Law into One's Hand in the Name of Commanding Good', the document goes on to state:

"Some fundamentalist and extremist groups gain power to achieve their political goals in the name of Commanding Good. For this, the Qur'anic injunction of helping others in the matters of good and piety is completely ignored. There is no doubt that it is imperative to forbid from evil but this has to be done through the people of wisdom. It is totally unacceptable in Islam that a certain group takes law into its own hands, declares people infidels, starts killing them in the name of commanding good and forbidding from evil."

"These trends, in any given society, lead to anarchy and chaos. Islam has clearly set the path for commanding good and forbidding bad by upholding the rule of law. Only the State has right to implement punishments on citizens and regulate their characters in accordance with law. It is necessary to revive the institutions of muwakhat and mu'amlat that were established at the time of Prophet Muhammad (peace be upon him) to promote cooperation between people." [8]

In another place the document writes concerning terrorism:

"These days, in order to take revenge from one's opponent, extremists are conducting suicide attacks on innocent people and against general public. In accordance with the teachings of Islam, these acts fall under dual crime; suicide and killing of innocents. Suicide is prohibited (Haram) in Islam, Allah, the Almighty said in the Holy Qur'an:

'And make not your own hands contribute to (your) destruction; but do good; for Allah loveth those who do good.' (Qur'an 2:195)

Terrorism and suicide attacks have no place in Islamic history. Such cruel and inhumane attacks started in 1789 during French revolution but in 1973 they were declared crime as per International Law. In Ulama's opinion terrorism related crimes fall in the category of "hirabah" and those practicing it shall be punished according to the Holy Qur'an. [9]

One point needs to be clarified here. As mentioned earlier, it is necessary to have state permission and guidance especially in the case of offensive Jihad. The circumstances may, however, be somewhat different in the case of defensive Jihad. For example, if there is foreign aggression against one's country, then Defensive Jihad becomes mandatory. If the state machinery still exists, then Jihad will be done under the state's guidance. And if state machinery is no more effective, then Jihad will still be done by group(s) of people against the foreign aggression. But even under such circumstances the Islamic guidance regarding Jihad/war must be scrupulously observed.

The topic of combative Jihad is not complete without mention of Islamic guidance with respect to wars, which I have repeatedly made reference to. Before delving into the subject, it is worthwhile contextualizing the discussion by recalling the devastating potential of war.

DEVASTATIONS OF WAR

"There is an urge and rage in people to destroy, to kill, to murder, and until mankind, without exception, undergoes a great change, wars will be waged, everything that has been built up, cultivated and grown, will be destroyed and disfigured, after which mankind will have to begin all over again." Writing in May 1944, the 14-year-old Jewish Anne Frank expressed despair, a sentiment shared by many during World War II. [10]

The statistics of war are jarring. According to research by Chris Hedges published in his work 'What every person should know about war' [11], of the past 3,400 years, human beings have been entirely at peace for a meagre 268, or just 8 percent of recorded history. Estimates for the total number killed in wars throughout all of human history range from 150 million to 1 billion.

Other than soldiers, war proves extremely perilous for civilians. Between 1900 and 1990, 43 million soldiers died in wars. During the same period, 62 million civilians were killed. More than 34 million civilians died in World War II alone. One million died in North Korea. Hundreds of thousands were killed in South Korea, and 200,000 to 400,000 in Vietnam. In the wars of the 1990s, civilian deaths constituted between 75 and 90 percent of all war deaths.

Civilians caught in war are victims of scores of traumas. They are shot, bombed, raped, starved, and driven from their homes. During World War II, 135,000 civilians died in two days in the firebombing of Dresden. A week later, in Pforzheim, Germany, 17,800 people were killed in 22 minutes. In Russia, after the three-year battle of Leningrad, only 600,000 civilians remained in a city that had held a population of 2.5 million. One million were evacuated, 100,000 were conscripted into the Red Army, and 800,000 died. In April 2003, during the Iraq War, half of the 1.3 million civilians in Basra were trapped for days without food and water in temperatures exceeding 100 degrees Fahrenheit.

More than 2 million children were killed in wars during the 1990s. Three times that number were disabled or seriously injured. Twenty million children were displaced from their homes in 2001. Many were forced into prostitution. A large percentage of those will contract AIDS. Children born to mothers who are raped or forced into prostitution often become outcasts.

Dozens of genocides have taken place since World War I. The most devastating include those in the Soviet Union, where approximately 20 million were killed during Stalin's Great Terror (1930s); Nazi Germany, where 6 million Jews were killed in concentration camps along with 5 million or more Gypsies, Jehovah's Witnesses, and other "enemies of the German state" (1937-1945); Cambodia, where 1.7 million of the country's 7 million people were killed as a result of the actions of the Khmer Rouge (1975-1979); Bosnia, where 310,000 Muslims were killed (1992-1995); and Rwanda, where more than 1 million Tutsis and moderate Hutus were slaughtered over ten weeks in 1994.

During the final stage of World War II, the United States dropped atom bombs on the Japanese cities of Hiroshima and Nagasaki on 6th and 9th August 1945, respectively. These bombs were dropped with the consent of the United Kingdom as drawn in the Quebec Agreement. These two nuclear bombings killed at least 129,000 people, most of those were civilians as the bombs were purposefully dropped in the two cities.

This is the reality of war and the kind of destruction it is capable of bringing to humanity, combatants and non-combatants alike. Great, unthinkable atrocities are committed by warring nations both during and after the war.

RULES AND MORALITY OF WAR IN ISLAM

Tipu Sultan, also known as the Tiger of Mysore, was the Muslim ruler of the Kingdom of Mysore from 1782 to 1799 that which is now part of the present-day India. He opposed British rule in South India and played a major role in keeping the British forces away. He was one of the few rulers who challenged British India. It is said that a soldier once asked Tipu Sultan: "Is it everything is fair in Love and War..?" In an epic sentence Tipu Sultan replied: "It's an excuse of English people. Our tradition is that, whatever is to be done in love and war, should be fair …"

Being an armed conflict, war is essentially undesirable. Despite this, human history is abounding with wars. Many wars that are fought are unjustified; however, this is not to deny the legitimacy of occasions when war becomes necessary for defending a nation against foreign aggression or for the eradication of evil.

Islam being a practical religion therefore does not deny the existence of war. The religion of Islam that has guided people in all spheres of life, has also provided guidance to Muslim armies in order to minimize human suffering and the loss of property and other resources. Muslim armies are not allowed to commit whatever atrocity they feel like in the name of war; rather, they must adhere to a strict code of conduct.

A few years ago, Mufti Nazeer Ahmed, a Pakistani Muslim scholar and head of Binoria Research Academy at Jamia Binoria, Karachi, Pakistan, wrote a paper on the 'rules and morality of wars in Islam'. He wrote the original paper in Urdu which was later translated into English. I found his paper very useful in understanding the subject. Therefore, with his permission, I have included following portions of the English translation of his paper:

"The words 'Rules' and 'Morality' are associated with two separate spheres of action. Rules or Laws are based upon justice, whereas higher moral behavior is based upon mercy and benevolence. Justice denotes preserving equality and fairness; that is, if a person inflicts harm or commits tyranny against someone, then an investigation is to be undertaken to determine whether he or she is innocent or guilty before further action is taken as per the law."

"On the other hand, mercy and benevolence entail displaying kindness, forgiveness, tolerance, patience, and amnesty towards others...."

The books of Islamic Jurisprudence differentiate between the rules of law and the rules of higher moral values as 'Qadah' and 'Diyantia'. 'Qadah' encompasses areas governed by the law, whereas 'Diyantia' encompasses areas that are governed by higher moral and ethical values. For example, as per the law it is not an obligation on the wife to perform household work, but from the perspective of higher moral and ethical values, it is befitting for her to do so. The point to note here is that although the spheres of judicial law and higher moral values are separate, the end result obtained through them is the same, that is, a peaceful society free of evil."

"A point of consideration brought forward by lawmakers and rulers is what is to be given priority if there is an apparent clash between the law and higher moral values."

"The answer is that the law would be given precedence as it is aimed at the collective good of society, whereas, higher moral values are dependent upon the individual's own choice. Take for example: the removal of street hawkers and the forced purchase of land for the purpose of widening roads, where each party is made to sacrifice for the general good of society."

"Jihad itself is called 'Hasan Laghaira', and from the standpoint of higher moral standards, it would be considered an unfavorable venture, that is, 'Qabih Laena'. However, according to the laws of justice, Jihad is necessary to eradicate the evils of society and to nullify plots of malicious intent. Like Jihad, constructing jails, administering punishments, manufacturing arms, and becoming a nuclear nation may all be against higher moral standards, but these are necessary as per the rules of justice...."

"Justice and benevolence are both upheld by Islam even in the occasion of war. Justice in war has been described as using enough force against the enemy to squelch the turmoil, and nothing else besides...."

One of the principles of war in Islam is that one can only fight with those who are able to fight. Those who cannot or do not wish to fight, shall not be killed."

"Prophet Muhammad [S.A.W.W] said, 'Do not kill elderly people, children, the young and women.' (Reported in Sahih Muslim)

War has predominantly been a mechanism for revenge and victory its goal. Revenge is barbaric, comparable to a lion's comportment at the time of catching its prey. This was the customary behavior of conquerors while dealing with conquered nations. Before the advent of Islam, the Arabs and other 'civilized' nations used to treat defeated nations as tools to vent off their extreme feelings of revenge. Allama Ibn Jubair, author of Ramla Ibn Jubair, was an eye witness to the crusades. He writes: 'And these are horrifying sights that one can witness in the cities. Muslim prisoners are seen with leg cuffs and are made to perform extremely challenging tasks. Similarly, Muslim women also chained at their shins, are made to perform inhumane works which is unbearable to watch.'"

"A common practice among the Arabs was to tie prisoners of war and use them for target practicing (a practice known as Sabir bin Nabl). The Prophet Muhammad [S.A.W.W] strictly condemned and banned this practice. Hazrat Khalid bin Waleed's [R.A.A] son Hazrat Abdul Rehman tied four soldiers of the enemy and killed them in the same manner described. When Hazrat Abu Ayub Ansari [R.A.A] came to know about this, he said, "I have heard that the Prophet [S.A.W.W] prohibited target practicing on the enemy prisoner. By Allah! if it were even a chicken, I would not use it for target practicing." Upon hearing this, Hazrat Abdul Rehman felt ashamed and freed four slaves to atone for this act."

"The Arabs were so barbaric that they used to humiliate women prisoners by tearing off their clothes. Arab women would even dismember the fetuses of pregnant women and wear them around their necks like garlands. Islam enforced that the principles of justice and benevolence must be adhered to and all inhumane acts were subsequently banned. Thus, the purposeless wars once fought without any principles were transformed into principled wars and like acts of worship."

"The Arabs and the 'civilized' nations of the time used to make false promises and accords as a tool to deceive the enemy. In reality, they would never honor their commitments or agreements as they considered them meaningless to begin with. In the incident of Ba'yer Mauna (the well of Mauna), the infidels did not keep their promise and killed the Companions of the Prophet [S.A.W.W]. The Holy Quran states: 'They do not observe any bond or treaty with a believer; and they are the transgressors.' (Surah At Tauba, Chapter 9, Ayat 10) And in another place the Holy Quran states: '… since their oaths are nothing…' (Surah At Tauba, Chapter 9, Ayat 12)"

"The just way to deal with such unprincipled nations is to treat them in the manner they treat others. But even in this regard Islam has provided principles and regulations. Hazrat Huzaifa bin-nil-yaman [R.A.A] and his father were migrating to Madinah when the nonbelievers captured them. They set them free on the condition that they will not fight against them in the Battle of Badr. At the time of the Battle of Badr, when they both expressed their desire to fight, Prophet Muhammad [S.A.W.W] did not allow them to on account of the word that they had given to the nonbelievers."

"At the time of the Treaty of Hudaibiya, Abu Raffay had come as a spokesperson on behalf of the nonbelievers. He was so impressed with the Muslims that he accepted Islam and refused to go back to the nonbelievers. Prophet Muhammad [S.A.W.W] insisted that he go back as he was an emissary and holding an emissary was against the treaty. The Prophet [S.A.W.W] therefore asked him to return to the nonbelievers and to come back to him after some time."

"At the time of the same treaty, Hazrat Abu Jandal [R.A.A] came to Prophet Muhammad [S.A.W.W]. He was in chains and his body was covered with wounds. The Companions of the Prophet [S.A.W.W] were outraged and pained by the sight. Although this decision seemed inhumane, the Prophet [S.A.W.W] sent him back. Honoring the pledge and maintaining justice were more pressing considerations, and benevolence receded in comparison."

"Citizens of the conquered nation are either those directly related to the war like the ruling class and the army, or those indirectly linked with the war."

"Islam encourages the use of benevolent behavior with the latter group rather than the use of justice. At the battle of Khyber, a Jewish woman tried to poison the Prophet's [S.A.W.W] food but he forgave her. When Makkah was conquered by the Muslims, the leaders and elders of the Quraysh tribe were pardoned. In both these instances of the conquest of Khyber and the conquest of Makkah, the affected people were allowed to keep their property. The same practice was continued by Hazrat Umer [R.A.A] when he conquered Iraq and other neighboring areas. After weeks of discussion, Hazrat Umer [R.A.A] accepted the right of the locals on the conquered lands. These are all examples of benevolence which do not fall under the umbrella of justice."

"Throughout this discussion one should bear in mind that the option of showing benevolent behavior by the Muslim ruler is to the extent that there is no violation of justice. When justice is denied, benevolence will not prevail, whether it be for prisoners of war or for the citizens of conquered nations."

"According to Hadith narrators and historians, the number of the most sought after criminals during the conquest of Makkah was ten. Based upon the consensus of reporters, only four of them were killed. They were (1) Abdullah bin Khatal, (2) Muqees bin Sababah (3) Hawairis and (4) Qa'arebah."

"… There is no room for benevolence when it comes to administering a 'Hadd' punishment. … The question may be raised here that why were they not pardoned like the elders of the Arab tribes? Simply put, it is the discretion of the ruler whether he pardons or punishes someone. The decision depends upon his wise judgment considering the situation at hand. It is possible that in these cases, it was important to set an example to highlight the severity of their crimes, and hence their sentences were carried out."

"Similar was the case of a prisoner of the Battle of Badar, Uqba bin Abi Mueet, who was executed and his plea for mercy denied. Likewise, the incident of Urnayeen prompted justice as the perpetrators had committed Haraba (commonly translated as terrorism), and thus punishment was administered as stipulated by 'Hudood. As per the Quranic verse regarding Haraba, their execution was necessary and there was no option of forgiving them."

"Citizens of the defeated nation who directly took part in the fighting are called prisoners of war. For them, the Holy Quran states: 'So, when you encounter those who disbelieve, then (aim at) smiting the necks, until when you have broken their strength thoroughly, then tie fast the bond, (by making them captives). Then choose (to release them) either (as) a favour (shown to them), or (after receiving) ransom, until the war throws down its load of arms…' (Surah Muhammad, Chapter 47, Ayat 4) This verse of the Holy Quran implies that the following types of treatment can be given to prisoners of war:

1. Release them without taking any compensation (Fidya).

2. Take compensation (Fidya) and release them; for example, four thousand Dirhams were taken from the prisoners of war of the Battle of Badr.

3. Make them work and release them after a specified duration; for example, the educated prisoners of the Battle of Badr were asked to educate others. Zaid bin Saabit [R.A.A] learnt to read and write in this way.

4. Kill them.

5. Make them slaves.

6. Get Muslim prisoners released in their exchange."

"All the aforementioned possibilities are legally valid. The decision of which is to be implemented resides with the ruler. Practically speaking, Muslims have mostly resorted to those options that demonstrate benevolence and mercy. In rare cases of severe necessity, justice was given preference to balance the score. Thus, the general impact of the behavior of Muslims towards prisoners of war resulted in their training rather than punishment. In fact, till the time of Hazrat Umer Farooq [R.A.A], prisoners of war used to live as guests and even teachers in Muslim households. The source of motivation for displaying such behavior was the Holy Quran which states, "…and they give food, out of their love for Him (Allah), to the needy, and the orphan, and the captive, (saying to them,) .We feed you only for the sake of Allah; we have no intention of (receiving) either a return from you or thanks." (Surah ad-Dahr, Chapter 76, Ayat 8-9)"

"Similarly, the Companions of the Prophet [S.A.W.W] were instructed to act towards prisoners of war with kindness and respect. It is because of this exhortation that the Companions used to treat the prisoners as their guests. Abu Aziz, the brother of Mus'ab bin Zubair [R.A.A], says that he had been captured at the Battle of Badr and handed over to a Muslim who was an Ansaari. The Ansaari Muslim used to toil all day and at the end of the day, would provide Abu Aziz with wheat bread and only eat dates himself. Abu Aziz used to feel embarrassed and would refuse to take the bread, but he would insist as they were advised by Prophet Muhammad [S.A.W.W] to be courteous to their prisoners of war."

"Hazrat Abbas [R.A.A] was a prisoner of war who didn't even have proper clothing to wear. Many of the Companions of the Prophet [S.A.W.W] presented him their clothes, but since he was a tall man the offered clothes didn't fit him. Eventually, Abdullah bin Abi bin Salool, a Munaafiq (hypocrite), presented his clothes which fit Hazrat Abbas [R.A.A]. One of the prisoners of war, Sohail bin Umro, was known for his powerful and captivating orations against the Muslims. Hazrat Umer Farooq [R.A.A] was of the opinion that his tongue be cut off so that once he is freed, he cannot repeat his crime. The Prophet [S.A.W.W] rejected the suggestion by saying that if he deforms anyone by pulling off his tongue, then, Allah [s.w.t] would do the same to him by deforming his body parts, even though he is a Prophet."

"Similarly, when Haatim Tai's daughter was arrested, she was held in the corner of a mosque and kept with dignity and respect until she was sent back to Yemen."

"Although according to legal rules, land, property, and other spoils of war would come under the ownership of the Muslim army and state, in reality the Muslims demonstrated generosity and benevolence by declaring spoils of war to be only those assets that were used in the battleground or by the enemy government. Beyond these, any individual's property was not touched. In other words, only those things which were used directly by the enemy would be taken into possession by the Muslims; other things were considered loot and were therefore strongly desisted."

"Once, some soldiers pillaged some goats from a neighboring village on their way to Jihad and put them to cook in large pots. When Prophet Muhammad [S.A.W.W] came to know about this, he was disturbed by the news. He went to the site and overturned the pots."

"Similarly, after the triumph at Khyber, some soldiers went ahead and looted some of the palaces. A Jewish leader came to Prophet Muhammad [S.A.W.W] to complain about this. He asked the Prophet [S.A.W.W] whether it seemed suitable to him to have their donkeys slaughtered, their fruits eaten, and their women beaten. Prophet Muhammad [S.A.W.W] called Abdur Rehman bin Auf [R.A.A] and instructed him to gather everyone for prayer. Then the Prophet [S.A.W.W] instructed everyone not to commit any type of plundering."

"It should be noted that this looting was forbidden (by Islam) at a time when the primary purpose of war was considered looting. Prophet Muhammad [S.A.W.W] altered the mindset of his people, making them realize that war was a way of expressing obedience to Allah [s.w.t] and spreading the message of Islam. And gradually, like with the commandments related to wine and gambling, the extreme love for spoils of war was curbed.

The reason for this historical attachment to spoils of war was, as quoted by Abu Ali Qaali: "It was not acceptable to the Arabs that they would completely stop looting for three straight months as it was their source of earning." (The book of Al-Amali, Volume 1, page 6)"

"The Arabs' survival rested on goats, sheep, and camels through drinking their milk, eating their meat, and using their fur for making blankets and clothes. In the desert there was no other source of livelihood, and in fact this source was also rare and not affordable for everyone. Hence, the Arabs used to attack each other for the purpose of capturing herds of animals. The easiest loot was that of goats (Ghanum) and because of its prevalence, the term 'Ghaneemut' came to refer to loot. The Arabs' desire for this loot can be gauged by the fact that for a long time some Muslims thought this is a pious practice and one that is rewarded by Allah s.w.t. But Islam gradually changed this mindset."

"According to a Hadith quoted in Abu Dawood, one of the Companions of the Prophet [S.A.W.W] asked him, "O Prophet Muhammad! There is a person who wants to go on Jihad (Holy War) and also wants to get something (loot) out of it." The Prophet [S.A.W.W] said that he will not get any reward from Allah [s.w.t]. He went and shared the Prophet's [S.A.W.W] reply with others. The people told him maybe he had misunderstood what the Prophet [S.A.W.W] said. So he came back to ask again. He got the same reply. He came again and even the third time, the Prophet [S.A.W.W] gave him the same answer, that such a person will not get any reward from Allah [s.w.t]."

"In order to dispel this misunderstanding, Allah [s.w.t] revealed the following verses after the Battle of Badr: "Had there not been a decree from Allah that came earlier, a great punishment would have overtaken you because of what you have taken. So, eat of the spoils you have got, lawful and pure, and fear Allah. Surely, Allah is Most-Forgiving, Very-Merciful." (Surah Al Anfal, Chapter 8, Ayat 68-69)"

""…the following verse of the Holy Quran was revealed: "They ask you about the spoils. Say, The spoils are for Allah and the Messenger…" (Surah Al Anfal, Chapter 8, Ayat 1) This verse made it unequivocally clear to the Muslims that the State is the custodian of anything received as 'Ghaneemut' during battle. And the manner of its distribution is the State's discretion. As a result, the practice of looting after war eventually came to an end. Due to various verses of the Holy Quran, Muslims started to equate the looting of 'Ghaneemat' to a loss of reward in the Hereafter."

"Hazrat Wasila Bin al Asqa [R.A.A] was one of the Companions of the Prophet [S.A.W.W]. When the Prophet [S.A.W.W] was leaving for the Battle of Tabuk, he (the companion) did not have any possessions to enable him to take part in the battle. He went around the streets of Medina calling out and asking if there was anyone willing to provide him with some sort of transport in return for an equal share in the 'Ghaneemat' he receives. Upon hearing this, an Ansar made the necessary arrangements for Hazrat Wasila [R.A.A]."

"Upon his return, Hazrat Wasila [R.A.A], who had received numerous camels and other goods as part of his share of 'Ghaneemat', presented everything to the Ansar. The Ansar told him to keep it all as his intention was to earn reward in the Hereafter and he did not want to lessen it by taking any of the 'Ghaneemat'."

"It was the result of such Islamic teachings that the ownership of lands in conquered territories was left to the locals rather than being captured as 'Ghaneemat'. During his rule, Hazrat Umer Farooq [R.A.A] suggested that khiraj and Jizya tax should be imposed on the inhabitants of conquered lands and none of the lands should be taken over by the Muslims. This decision was fully supported by the Muslim army."

"War is inevitable for any nation to protect its sovereignty. …Unfortunately, wars have always resulted in barbarism and violence by the conquering nation, cultivating hatred, revulsion, aggression, and revenge in the eyes of the defeated. The vanquishers, intoxicated with the power of victory, have invariably ill-treated, abused, and played with the honor of the weakened state. Umro bin Hind, an Arab king who conquered Banu Tammim, was unable to control himself in his fervor of revenge and went to the extent of burning alive an innocent old lady. Using enemy skulls as glasses to have wine and dismembering unborn fetuses to use as garlands, were common practices of the time. Islam, while regarding war as a necessity of sovereign nations, has contained it within the boundaries of justice and morality. Rules were prescribed (by Islam) for wars as a result of which wars were fought in the same respectful and dutiful manner as prayers were offered, fasts were observed, and Hajj was performed. Arrogance and conceitedness were frowned upon and kindness and compassion were instructed."

"As stated in the Holy Quran: 'O you who believe, when you face a group (in battle), stand firm and remember Allah abundantly, so that you may be successful. Obey Allah and His Messenger, and do not quarrel with each other, lest you should lose courage, and your prowess should evaporate; and be patient. Surely, Allah is with the patient. And do not be like those who set forth from their homes waxing proud and showing off to people, preventing (people) from the way of Allah. Allah is All-Encompassing of what they do.' (Surah Al-Anfal, Chapter 8, Ayat 45-47)"

"The day Prophet Muhammad [S.A.W.W] entered Makkah as a victor with a large Muslim army, out of his modesty and humbleness, he held his head so low that his forehead was touching the hump of his camel. On the day of the conquest of Khyber, he rode an ordinary donkey using a slice of a bark of date tree instead of a proper rein. The result of such rectifications and refinements was that war became a source of restoring peace and a great means of spreading Islam and the Word of Allah [s.w.t]. The negative aspects of war started to disappear, and the positive ones started to become evident. As a result, common people used to motivate Muslims to attack their states and would help them during battles."

"Here I would like to quote an excerpt from Dr. Hameed Ullah's book: 'In the beginning, the state of Madina was a city state. It was not even a complete city, as it was established on a portion of the city. Later it underwent rapid expansion. You can judge its rate of expansion by the fact that in just ten years following the death of Prophet Muhammad [S.A.W.W], it was no longer just a city state but rather the capital of a massive empire. According to historical facts, the total area of this vast empire was approximately 3 million square kilometers. In other words, it expanded with an average rate of eight hundred forty-five square kilometers per day. Such an expansion was partly peaceful and partly achieved with the help of war. We have figures for the other wars as well in addition to the number of people killed or martyred during the time of Prophet Muhammad [S.A.W.W] during the wars of 'Ghazawat' and 'Saraya'."

"In order to conquer a land of three million square kilometers, the rate of killing among enemy lines was not even two per month. There are one hundred and twenty months in ten years, doubling this figure amounts to two hundred and forty. Even this many people were not killed. The total number of enemies killed was less than this figure, and the Muslims martyred even fewer. The biggest loss occurred during Ghazwa-i-Uhad during which seventy Muslims were martyred. And this loss was also due to a mistake made by the Muslims. The point to note here is that the rate of enemies killed in battlefields was even less than two per month." (Khutbat-i-Bahawalpur, page 206, publisher Idara-i-Tahqeeqat-i-Islami)"

"As stated, war is a necessity for a sovereign nation. According to Jewish teachings, the only principle of civilized war is 'Justice'. In the Christian tradition there is no mention of war at all. The focus of the teachings of Christianity is moral values. Thus, there is neither mention of retaliation nor of justice as counter-measures against enemy aggression. Islam, which is a beautiful combination of justice and moral values, guides us towards the establishment of peace and a system of justice in society. Islam, considering wars inevitable for sovereign nations, admits their existence but attaches to them principles of justice and morality, thereby curbing the ghastly effects of wars. Wars without any checks and balances of justice and morality are considered barbarism by Islam."

"In the language of the civilized world, war without principles is nothing but barbarism, whereas war accompanied with the principles of justice and morality is based on higher human values. Today's professedly humane and developed civilizations have failed to assign moral values a place in wars. Islam has given priority to moral values over justice even in war, and this is not limited to theory only. Islam has furthered the concept through legislation and the provision of spiritual training so that a Muslim soldier does not fight with a vindictive attitude against his deadly enemy on the battleground. Rather he bases his conduct upon moral values. While it may be difficult to conceive, Islam has practically demonstrated it."

"Allah [s.w.t] says in Quran: "…Today, I have perfected your religion for you, and have completed My blessing upon you, and chosen Islam as Deen (religion and a way of life) for you…" (Surah Al-Maida, Chapter 5, Ayat 3)"

CONCLUDING REMARKS

Despite commendable progress in the field of science and technology, the world is rife with tyranny, exploitation, and injustice. It has justifiably been said that man has learned to fly like a bird and swim like a fish but has not yet learned to live like a human being.

I hope this book has provided you with valuable knowledge and information to fully comprehend the issue of extremism and terrorism in the world. I am hopeful that you are now in a better position to judge whether to blame the religion of Islam for terrorism or those involved in these acts of terrorism. It is also wrong to mix the concepts of Jihad and terrorism. In fact, no religion in the world can sanction or approve of such violence and unjustified killing of the innocent. On the other hand, it is evident from the data that acts of terrorism are largely motivated by the political objectives of the perpetrators.

We must also try to disseminate the message among nations that there are certain rules of morality that must be complied with even during war. Bombing civilians, raping women, torturing people, using weapons of mass destruction on non-combatant populations, etc., are all examples of immoral practices that are commonplace even in today's 'civilized' world.

As Noam Chomsky succinctly put it "Everybody's worried about stopping terrorism. Well, there's a really easy way: stop participating in it." [1] States must recognize that their acts of sponsoring terrorism in enemy states bring about enormous human suffering. While the general population of a country usually has nothing to do with their state's policies. Many countries need to get out of such hypocritical mindset. of making a hue and cry over terrorism and at the same time sponsoring terrorism in other states.

All nations should recognize that it is their joint responsibility to make the world a safer place to live. They should also learn to resolve political disputes in a peaceful manner using forums like the United Nations. Such platforms also need to be made more effective for the future.

APPENDICES

APPENDIX A: ISLAM A RELIGION OF PEACE?

Shortly after an attack on May 22, 2013, on a British soldier in London, the Oxford Union society held a debate on the motion: This house believes Islam is a religion of peace. During the debate, the arguments against Islam by Anne-Marie Waters and Daniel Johnson were devastated by the responses Mehdi Hassan gave to their diatribe against Islam and Muslims. I am reproducing the complete text of the interesting speech delivered by Mr. Mehdi Hasan during the debate which is very useful in understanding the topic of terrorism and Islam:

Mehdi Hassan: Thank you very much Mr. President, ladies and gentlemen, good evening. As-salaamu alaykum, lovely to see you all here tonight. We are having a very entertaining night, are we not? With some very interesting things been said from the other side of the House tonight. Let me begin by saying, as a Muslim, as a representative of Islam, I would consider myself an ambassador for Islam, a believer in Islam, a follower of Islam and its prophet—so in that capacity—let me begin by apologizing to Anne-Marie for the Bali bombings. I apologize for the role of my religion, and me and my people for the killing of Theo van Gogh, 7/7... Yes, that was all of us. That was Islam, that was Muslims, that was the Qur'an. I mean, astonishing, astonishing claims to make in the very first speech on a day like today, where the Conservative PM of the United Kingdom has to come out and point out that these kind of views are anathema. And I believe you are trying to stand for the Labour Party, to become an MP in Brighton. If you do, and you make these comments, I'm guessing you'll have the whip withdrawn from you, but then again, UKIP are on the rise, they'll take you, the BNP, they might have something to say about your views.

Anne-Marie Waters: This is...This is what Mehdi Hasan always does!

Mehdi Hassan: By the way, just on the factual points, as we heard a lot, from the second speaker about how backward we Muslims all are, on a factual point, you said that Islam was born in Saudi Arabia. Islam was born in 610 AD, Saudi Arabia was born in 1932 AD, so you were only 1,322 years off. Not bad, not bad start there.

Talking of maths, by the way, a man called Al-Khwarizmi, one of the greatest mathematicians of all time, a Muslim, worked in the Golden Age of Islam, he's the guy who came out with not just algebra but algorithms.

Without algorithms, you wouldn't have laptops, and without laptops, Daniel Johnson today wouldn't have been able to print out his speech in which he came to break us Muslims for holding back the advance and intellectual achievements of the West, which all happened without any contributions from anyone else other than the Judeo Christian people of Europe. In fact, Daniel Davin Levering the author of the Pulitzer Prize, winning historian and author of the "Golden Prism of Winter", that there would be no renaissance, no reformation in Europe without the role played by Ibn Sina and Ibn Rushd, some of the great Muslim theologians, philosophers, scientists, in bringing these texts to Europe. □

(Applause)

Mehdi Hassan: As for this being "our" university, I will leave that to the imagination as to who is "our" and who is "their", I studied here, too. An astonishing, astonishing set of speeches so far making this case tonight. A mixture of just cherry-picked quotes, facts and figures self-serving, selective, a farrago of distortions, misrepresentations, misinterpretations, misquotations. Daniel talked about my article in the "New Statesman" which got me a lot of flak where I talked about the anti-semitism that is prevalent in some parts of Muslim community, which indeed it is. Of course, I didn't say in that piece it was caused by the religion of Islam, in fact, modern anti-semitism in the Middle East was imported from—finish the sentence—Christians! Judeo Christian Europe, where I believe some certain bad things happened to the Jewish people. In fact, Tom Friedman, a Jewish American columnist in "The New York Times", told me in this very Chamber last week that he believed had Muslims been running Europe in the 1940s, 6 million extra Jews would still be alive today. So I am not going to take lessons in anti-semitism from someone who's here to defend the Judeo Christian values of a continent that murdered 6 million Jews...Moving swiftly on. Moving swiftly on.

(Groans from audience)

Anne-Marie Waters: Unbelievable.

(Audience) And you are doing exactly—

Anne-Marie Waters: Absolutely.

Mehdi Hassan:—No, no, no, no! I'm about to make a point. You're right! I agree with you! I agree with you 110%! That is my point. I don't think Europe is evil or bad. I'm a very proud European. I don't want to judge Europe on this. But if we are going to play this gutter game where we pull out the Bali bombings, and we pull out examples of anti-semitism of Islam, then of course I will come back and say, "Hold on." I mean, look, let's be very clear. Daniel here was a last minute replacement for Douglas Murray who had to pull out, and Douglas and I have very well documented differences, but to be fair to Douglas, as to be fair to Anne-Marie, and to Peter, atheists.

Atheists see all religions as evil, violent, threatening. The problem I have with Daniel's speech is that Daniel comes here to run this robust defense of Christianity forgetting that his fellow Christians, people who said that they were acting in the name of Jesus gave us the Crusades, the Spanish Inquisition, the Anti Jewish Pogroms, European colonialism in Africa and Asia, the Lord's Resistance Army in Uganda, not to mention countless arson and bomb attacks on abortion clinics in the United States of America till this very day. I would like a little bit of humility from Daniel first, before he begins lecturing other communities and other faiths on violence, terror, and intolerance.

(Applause)

Mehdi Hassan: But... No, thank you. (A glass of water.) But I would say this: to address the gentleman's very valid point here, I am not going to play that game. I don't actually believe that Christianity is a religion of violence and hate, because of what the LRA does in Uganda, or what the Crusaders did to Jews and Muslims in Jerusalem when they took back the city in the 12th or 13th, or whatever century it was. I believe that Christianity, like Islam, like pretty much every mainstream religion is based on love, and compassion, and faith.

I do follow a religion in which 113 out of 114 chapters of the Qur'an begins by introducing the God of Islam as the God of mercy, and compassion. I would not have it any other way. I don't follow a religion which introduces my God to me as a god of war, as some kind of Greek god of wrath, as a god of hate and injustice. Not at all. As Adam pointed out, you go through the Qu'ran and you see the mercy, and the love, and the justice. And yes, you have verses that refer to warfare, and violence. Of course it does, this is not a motion about pacifism. I am not here to argue that Islam is a pacifistic faith. It is not.

Islam allows military action, and violence in certain limited context, and yes, a minority of Muslims do take it out of that context. But is it religious? We talked about Woolwich; Daniel and Anne-Marie have suggested that it is definitely religion that is behind all of this.

Mehdi Hassan: Well, actually, what I find so amusing tonight is we have a debate about Islam, and the opposition tonight has come forward, we have a graduate in Law, one in Modern History, in Chemistry, and you know, I admire all of their intellects and abilities but we don't have anyone who's actually an expert on Islam, a scholar of Islam, a historian of Islam, a speaker of Arabic, even a terrorism or a security expert, or a pollster, let alone to talk about about what Muslims believe or think. Instead, we have people coming here putting forward these views, putting forward these sweeping opinions. Listen to Professor Robert Pape of the University of Chicago, one of America's leading terrorism experts, who, unlike our esteemed opposition tonight, studied every single case of suicide terrorism between 1980 and 2005. 315 cases in total. And he concluded, and I quote: "There is little connection between suicide terrorism and Islamic fundamentalism or any of the world's religions. Rather, what nearly all suicide terrorist attacks have in common is a specific secular and strategic goal to compel modern democracies to withdraw military forces from territories that the terrorists consider to be their homeland." And the irony is, when we talk about terrorism, the irony is that the opposition and the Muslim terrorists, the Al-Qaeda types, actually have one thing in common, because they both believe that Islam is a war-like, violent religion. They both agree on that.

They have everything in common. Osama Bin Laden would be nodding along to everything that was said tonight by the opposition, he agrees with them.

(Applause)

Mehdi Hassan: The problem is that mainstream Muslims don't, the majority of Muslims around the world don't, in fact a gentleman that started quoting all sorts of polls, Gallup, carried out the biggest poll of Muslims around the world, of 50,000 Muslims in 35 countries, 93% of Muslims rejected 9/11 and suicide attacks, and of the 7% who didn't, they all, when polled in focus groups cited political reasons for their support for violence not religious reasons.

As for Islamist scholars and what they say, well, Daniel talks about "our" University of Oxford; well, go down to "Oxford Center for Islamic Studies", get hold of a man named Shaykh Afifi al-Akiti who's a massively well credentialed and well-respected Islamic scholar, who has studied across the world, who in the days after the 7/7, published a fatwa denouncing terrorism in the name of Islam, calling for the protection of all non-combatants at all times, and describing suicide bombings as an innovation with no basis in Islamic law. Go and listen to Shaykh Tahir-ul-Qadri, one of Pakistan's most famous Islamic scholars who published a 600-page fatwa condemning the killing of all innocents in all suicide bombings unconditionally without any ifs or buts. There's nothing new here; this is mainstream Islam, mainstream scholarship which has said this for years: you don't go out and kill people willy-nilly in the high street or anywhere else, on a bus or a mall based on verses of the Qur'an you cherry-picked without any context, any understanding, any interpretation or any commentary.

(Audience) [inaudible]

Mehdi Hassan: Please.

(Audience) What's that solely [inaudible]

Mehdi Hassan: I didn't say it doesn't happen at all. I never said it didn't happen. I don't blame Islam. Yes. It's a very good point. And a lot of us, are campaigning against that. I am campaigning against it in the name of Islam. We are campaigning against it in the name of various interpretations of Islam. Anne-Marie comes and scares us with her talk of Sharia Law, I would like to see the book of Sharia Law, it doesn't exist. People argue about what the Sharia Law is and you empower the extremists by saying there is only one version. You empower them all. I don't believe you took any interruptions Anne-Marie...

Anne-Marie Waters: Several [inaudible]

Mehdi Hassan: So I think you should stay there for a moment.

Mehdi Hassan: Here's what we are dealing with—

Anne-Marie Waters: Several [inaudible]

Mehdi Hassan:—I took your point. Here's what we are dealing with: a 1400 year old global religion followed by 1.6 billion people in every corner of the world, a quarter of humanity, of all backgrounds, cultures, ethnicities, and yet, the oppositions tonight wants to generalise, stereotype, smear, in order to desperately win these debates.

And here's my question if we're going to generalise and smear: if, okay, people say yesterday's bombers and we've got to be careful there's a trial going on, were yesterday attackers sorry, motivated by Islam, big debate, I don't believe they were, let's say they were, let's say Faisal Shahzad, The Time Square bomber was motivated by Islam, let's assume for the sake of the argument that Richard Reid the shoe bomber was motivated by Islam, if Islam is responsible for this killings, if it is what is motivating these people, and it's therefore not a religion of peace then ask yourself this question: why aren't the rest of us doing it?

Why is it such a tiny minority of Muslims who are interpreting their religion in the way that the opposition claim they are? Let's assume there are 16,000 suicide bombers in the world—there aren't—let's assume there are for the sake of argument.

That 0.001 percent of the Muslims population globally, what about the other 99.99% of Muslims who the opposition tonight either ignore or smear? The reality is that the rest of us aren't blowing ourselves up tonight, the reality is that the opposition came in tonight not worried about the fact that me and Adam might pull open a jacket and blow ourselves up tonight because we are followers of warlike, warrior religion which want to take over Europe and Daniel's university. The issue is this...

(Laughter)

(Applause)

Mehdi Hassan:—unless the opposition can tell us tonight, and Peter Atkins is here, one of our great atheist intellectuals can tell us tonight, can they answer this question tonight: why don't the vast majority of Muslims around the world behave as violently and aggressively as the tiny minority of politically motivated extremists? Then they might as well give up and stop pretending they have anything relevant to say about Islam or Muslims as a whole.

Ladies and gentlemen, let me just say this to you: think about what the opposite of this motion is. If you vote no tonight, what you'll say the opposite of this motion is: that Islam isn't a religion of peace, it's a religion of war, of violence, of terror, of aggression.

That the people who follow Islam, me, my wife, my retired parents, my 6 year old child, that 1.8 million of your fellow British residents and citizens, that 1.6 billion people across the world, your fellow human beings, are all followers, promoters, believers in a religion of violence. Do you really think that? Do you really believe that to be the case?

Mehdi Hassan: They say that in Oxford Union, the most famous debate was in 1933 when Adolf Hitler looked out for the result of the King and Country motion, where they voted against fighting for the King and country and Hitler was listening up for the result. Well, tonight, 80 years on, there are two groups of people around the world who, I would argue, are waiting for the results of tonight's vote:

there are the millions of peaceful, non-violent, law-abiding Muslims in the UK, Europe, Asia, Africa and beyond, who see Islam as the source of their identity, spiritual fulfilment, hope and solace, and then there are the phobes, the haters, the bigots out there who want to push the clash of civilisations, who want to divide all of us into them, and us, and ours, and theirs.

Ladies and gentlemen, I urge you all not to fuel the arguments of the phobes and bigots, don't legitimise their division, don't legitimise their hate, trust those Muslims who you know, who you've met, who you hear, who don't believe in violence, who do want you to hear the peaceful message of the Qur'an, as they believe it to be taught to the majority of Muslims, the Islam of peace, and compassion, and mercy, the Islam of the Qur'an, not of Al-Queda. Ladies and gentlemen, I beg to propose this motion to the House, I urge you to vote yes tonight. Thank you very much for your time.

(Applause) [1]

Finally, the motion that "This house believes Islam is a religion of peace" was won by majority votes.

APPENDIX B: OTHER BOOKS BY ADEEL ZEERAK

Islam: A Superior System of Life

CreateSpace (306 pp.); September 10, 2012

ISBN: 1-4775-1710-3

ISBN-13: 978-1-4775-1710-9

One of the largest and fastest-growing religions, Islam is currently practiced by approximately one-fifth of the world's population. Unlike most religions that only consist of acts of worship, rituals, and a set of beliefs, it also offers a just socio-politico-economic system, which is especially important today as we continue to make significant material and scientific progress. However, although it presents real solutions to problems faced by the whole of mankind, factors such as worldwide media propaganda and the current condition of the Muslim community have seriously distorted the public image of Islam. Adeel Zeerak hopes that his book Islam: A Superior System of Life will help change all that.

He says that after careful study, even those with non-Muslim unprejudiced minds will appreciate the beauty of his religion's teachings. To prove the superiority of Islamic system over other systems, he provides concrete data obtained from authentic sources and refrains from using boastful or exaggerative language. Chapters in Islam: A Superior System of Life includes:

1. This is Islam

2. Characteristics of the Islamic System

3. Spiritual System

4. Social System

5. Economic System

6. Political System

7. The Prophet, peace be upon him, the Message, and the Ummah

"Despite commendable progress in the field of science and technology, this world is full of evil, exploitation, and injustice," says Zeerak, who believes any effort to find a solution to our problems continually fails because we choose to ignore the light of Divine Guidance. We all know what happened to Prophet Noah's people when they rejected this guidance, but we, thankfully, still exist in this world to follow our Lord and accept Islam.

Written for the Muslim and non-Muslim, Islam: A Superior System of Life is for readers interested in Islam, the Prophet Muhammad (PBUH), the Islamic view of women, the concept of Khilafat, Islamic finance, Islamic spirituality, and Islamic history. The author promises that our obedience to Allah, subhanahu wa-ta'ala, will result in endless favors and blessings both in this world and the hereafter.

"The book's greatest success is that it presents Islam as a dynamic, adaptive, and ultimately humanitarian, faith that has something to offer followers in every aspect of their daily lives. In this way, it amends much of the false and reductive rhetoric that has been applied to the faith in the wake of 9/11."

KIRKUS INDIE REVIEW

Women, Feminism, and Islam

CreateSpace (194 pp.); April 12, 2014

ISBN: 1-4922-3550-4

ISBN 13: 978-1-4922-3550-7

If asked for your perspective of Islam's treatment of women, what would you say?

How would you explain Western feminism?

Many Westerners believe that Islamic teachings are anti-woman, when the truth is that the religion gave many rights to women centuries before the rest of the world, including education, ownership and control of property, inheritance, and freedom of expression.

Many Muslims believe that Western feminism is mostly the promotion of vulgarity and immorality, but it is actually an ongoing movement in pursuit of equal rights between genders.

In Women, Feminism, and Islam, Adeel Zeerak provides secular and Islamic explorations of women's roles in society, exploitation, and rights. He discusses why gender equity is a better term to use than gender equality, differentiates the terms liberation and debauchery for people, and details how anti-women practices found in some Muslim regions are not at all related to Islam.

This compelling discourse breaks down the wall of assumptions and stereotypes, through balanced, research-based discussion that is both enlightening and educational. By its end, you may find yourself wondering what other misperceptions are clouding your views and judgments of the rest of the diverse world population.

"A worthwhile read that corrects several misconceptions."

KIRKUS INDIE REVIEW

NOTES

Chapter 1: Terrorism – A Global Menace

1   This quotation is taken from the internet website: www.brainyquote.com.

2   Farid Sabri, "67,399 people killed in terror attacks during past 15 years," <u>Pakistan Today</u>, May 20, 2017
(https://www.pakistantoday.com.pk/2017/05/20/67399-people-killed-in-terror-attacks-during-past-15-years/)

3   Melanie Phillips, <u>Londonistan</u>, Encounter Books, New York, 2006

4   Shawna Ayoub Ainslie, "20 Ways 9/11 changed my life as an (American) Muslim," <u>Huffington Post</u>, December 6, 2017
(https://www.huffingtonpost.com/shawna-ayoub-ainslie/20-ways-911-changed-my-life_b_8111518.html)

5   Oren Dorell, "Islamic State made Ramadan 2016 bloodiest ever," <u>USA Today</u>, July 7, 2016
(https://www.usatoday.com/story/news/world/2016/07/07/islamic-state-made-ramadan-2016-bloodiest-ever/86815532/Oren Dorell)

6   https://twitter.com/justintrudeau/status/749623836937596928?lang=en

7   Training manual, <u>Politics, Media and War: 9/11 and its aftermath</u>, The Open University, UK, 2016, pp. 15
(Internet link: http://www.open.edu/openlearn/free-courses/full-catalogue)

8   One such book is <u>9/11 The Big Lie</u> written by Thierry Meyssan. Published in 2002 by Carnot Publishing Ltd, London, UK, the book challenges the entire official version of the 9/11 terrorist attacks.

Chapter 2: Understanding Extremism and Terrorism

1   This quotation is taken from the internet website: www.brainyquote.com.

2   https://www.merriam-webster.com/words-at-play/history-of-the-word-terrorism?src=defrecirc-peoplearereading-sans-serif

3 https://en.oxforddictionaries.com/definition/terrorism

4 https://www.merriam-webster.com/dictionary/terrorism

5 Training manual, <u>Politics, Media and War: 9/11 and its aftermath</u>, The Open University, UK, 2016, pp. 25
(Internet link: http://www.open.edu/openlearn/free-courses/full-catalogue)

6 https://en.wikipedia.org/wiki/Terrorism

7 Training manual, <u>Politics, Media and War: 9/11 and its aftermath</u>, The Open University, UK, 2016, pp. 26
(Internet link: http://www.open.edu/openlearn/free-courses/full-catalogue)

8 https://www.fbi.gov/investigate/terrorism

9 https://en.oxforddictionaries.com/definition/terrorism

10 https://www.merriam-webster.com/dictionary/terrorism

11 https://en.wikipedia.org/wiki/Extremism

12 http://www.terrorism-research.com/goals/

13 Colleen Curry, "Christians and Muslims Face More Persecution by Hindu Extremists in India," <u>Vice News</u>, March 17, 2016.

(https://news.vice.com/article/christian-and-muslims-are-facing-more-and-more-persecution-by-hindu-extremists-in-india)

14 https://www.alternet.org/tea-party-and-right/10-worst-terror-attacks-extreme-christians-and-far-right-white-men

15 Hannah Beech, "Extremist Buddhist Monks Target Religious Minorities," <u>TIME</u>, June 20, 2013

(http://world.time.com/2013/06/20/extremist-buddhist-monks-fight-oppression-with-violence/)

16   "Rohingya crisis: At least 6,700 Rohingya Muslims killed in one month, says Doctors Without Borders," <u>Independent</u>, December 14, 2017

(http://www.independent.co.uk/news/world/asia/rohingya-crisis-latest-6700-muslims-killed-two-months-burma-doctors-without-borders-persecution-a8109131.html)

17   Giles Fraser, "It's not religion that create terrorists, it's the politics," <u>The Independent</u>, June 27, 2015

(https://www.theguardian.com/commentisfree/belief/2015/jun/27/its-not-the-religion-that-creates-terrorists-its-the-politics)

18   Lowenheim, <u>Predators and Parasites: Persistent Agents of Transnational Harm and Great Power Authority</u>, The University of Michigan Press, 2007.

19   http://www.terrorism-research.com/goals/

20   Ben Dupre, <u>50 Political Ideas you really need to know</u>, Quercus, London, 2010, pp. 159

21   Dean Nelson, "Chuck Hagel criticised for India-Afghanistan remarks," <u>The Telegraph</u>, February 27, 2013

(http://www.telegraph.co.uk/news/worldnews/asia/india/9897707/Chuck-Hagel-criticised-for-India-Afghanistan-remarks.html)

22
https://www.researchgate.net/publication/309462454_Indian_Influence_in_Afghanistan_and_its_Implications_for_Pakistan

23   "India and the Baloch Insurgency," <u>The Hindu</u>, March 12, 2010

(http://www.thehindu.com/todays-paper/tp-opinion/India-and-the-Baloch-insurgency/article16564162.ece)

24   "Full text of Kubhushan Jadhav's confession," <u>The Hindu</u>, April 10, 2017

(http://www.thehindu.com/news/national/full-text-of-kulbhushan-jadhavs-confession/article17907019.ece)

25 Training manual, <u>Politics, Media and War: 9/11 and its aftermath</u>, The
    Open University, UK, 2016, pp. 33
(Internet link: http://www.open.edu/openlearn/free-courses/full-catalogue)

Chapter 3: Islam and Terrorism

1 This quotation is taken from the internet website: www.thinkexist.com.

2 Dr. Mufti Abdul Wahid, <u>Masail-i-Bihishti Zewar vol. 1</u>, (Karachi: Majlis-i-
Nasharyat-i-Islam, 2007), pp. 30 - 31.

3 G. A. Parwez, "Genesis and ideology of Pakistan".

4 Mufti Muhammad Taqi Usmani, <u>An introduction to Islamic Finance</u>,
(Karachi: Maktaba Ma'ariful Quran, 2002), pp. 15 – 16.

5 Adeel Zeerak, <u>Islam: A Superior System of Life</u>, (USA: Createspace, 2012).
This book is available at www.Amazon.com.

6 These statements are taken from: http://kurzman.unc.edu/islamic-
statements-against-terrorism/

7 MSANews, September 14, 2001 (via archive.org).
Arabic original in al-Quds al-Arabi (London), September 14, 2001, p. 2 (via
archive.org).

8 The Dawn newspaper, Karachi, Pakistan, February 8, 2003 (via
archive.org); also in "Public Statements by Senior Saudi Officials
Condemning Extremism and Promoting Moderation," May 2004, page 10 (via
archive.org).

9 Harun Yahya, Islam Denounces Terrorism, (New York: Tahrike Tarsile
Quran, Inc, 2002)

10 The New York Times, September 28, 2001, p. B3.

11 British Muslim Forum, press release of July 18, 2005 (via archive.org).

12http://www.slate.com/blogs/the_slatest/2014/09/25/muslims_scholars_open_letter_to_isis_baghdadi_caliphate_s_actions_against.html

13 "MI5 report challenges views on terrorism in Britain," <u>The Guardian,</u> November 6, 2015

https://www.theguardian.com/uk/2008/aug/20/uksecurity.terrorism1

14 Roy, Olivier, "What is the driving force behind jihadist terrorism?", <u>Inside Story</u>, 18 December 2015. Inside Story.

(http://insidestory.org.au/what-is-the-driving-force-behind-jihadist-terrorism/)

15 Lilla, Mark, France: Is There a Way Out?

 http://www.nybooks.com/articles/2016/03/10/france-is-there-a-way-out/

16 https://abbtakk.tv/en/army-releases-confessional-statement-of-surrendered-ttp-spokesman-ehsanullah-ehsan-26-04-2017/

17 http://dunyanews.tv/en/Pakistan/320212-India-Afghanistan-direct-terrorism-in-Pakistan-L

18 "Parsons Green Bomber ….," <u>Independent</u>, March 23, 2018

(https://www.independent.co.uk/news/uk/crime/parsons-green-bomber-ahmed-hassan-sentence-terror-attack-prison-sentence-life-guilty-a8270556.html)

Chapter 4: Political Connection

1 This quotation is taken from the internet website: www.brainyquote.com.

2   Giles Fraser, "It's not the religion that creates terrorists, it's the politics," The Guardian, June 27, 2015

(https://www.theguardian.com/commentisfree/belief/2015/jun/27/its-not-the-religion-that-creates-terrorists-its-the-politics)

3   Henry Schuster, CNN, 30 June 2005.

(http://edition.cnn.com/2005/WORLD/meast/06/30/schuster.column/)

4   Training manual, Politics, Media and War: 9/11 and its aftermath, The Open University, UK, 2016, pp. 28
(Internet link: http://www.open.edu/openlearn/free-courses/full-catalogue)

5   Ibid, pp. 29

6   "Text: Osama Bin Laden's 1998 interview," The Guardian, October 8, 2001

(https://www.theguardian.com/world/2001/oct/08/afghanistan.terrorism15
)

7   Alexandra Wilts, "Donald Trump recognizing Jerusalem as Israel's capital will cause major catastrophe, Middle East leaders warn," Independent, December 4, 2017

(http://www.independent.co.uk/news/world/americas/us-politics/trump-jersualem-israel-capital-violence-unrest-threat-warning-middle-east-latest-a8091766.html)

8   "UN votes resoundingly to reject Trump's recognition of Jerusalem as capital," The Guardian, December 21, 2017

(https://www.theguardian.com/world/2017/dec/21/united-nations-un-vote-donald-trump-jerusalem-israel)

9   Ben Dupre, 50 Political Ideas you really need to know, Quercus, London, 2010, pp. 104.

10 Training manual, <u>Politics, Media and War: 9/11 and its aftermath</u>, The
    Open University, UK, 2016, pp. 56
(Internet link: http://www.open.edu/openlearn/free-courses/full-catalogue)

11 Ibid, pp. 47

12 Ibid, pp. 48

13 https://defence.pk/pdf/threads/us-created-taliban-and-abandoned-
pakistan-says-hillary.434287/

14 http://www.al-monitor.com/pulse/politics/2014/09/turkey-usa-iraq-
syria-isis-fuller.html#ixzz54RwH1iyv

15 https://www.youtube.com/watch?v=mCHuZM_9qTk

16 Jason Hanna, <u>CNN</u>, 13 August 2016.
(http://edition.cnn.com/2016/08/12/middleeast/here-is-how-isis-
began/index.html)

17 <u>Al Jazeera</u>, 10 November 2017.

(http://www.aljazeera.com/news/2017/11/hamid-karzai-colluded-isil-
afghanistan-171110191715544.html)

18 https://www.youtube.com/watch?v=YCedWxlG90M

19 Training manual, <u>Politics, Media and War: 9/11 and its aftermath</u>, The
    Open University, UK, 2016, pp. 65
(Internet link: http://www.open.edu/openlearn/free-courses/full-catalogue)

20 Dalia Mogahed, "This is the face of a terrorist: White people must
understand the damage done by group blame that follows other terror
attacks," <u>Daily News</u>, March 21, 2018

(http://www.nydailynews.com/opinion/face-terrorist-article-1.3888551)

21   Herman, E.S. and Chomsky, N, <u>Manufacturing Consent: the political economy of the mass media,</u> (London: Vintage, 1994), pp. 19 – 23.

22   Aliyah Frumin and Amanda Sakma, <u>NBC News,</u> 11 September 2016. (https://www.nbcnews.com/storyline/9-11-anniversary/hope-despair-being-muslim-america-after-9-11-n645451)

23 Yonette Joseph, " 'Punish a Muslim Day' Letters Rattle U.K. Communities," <u>The New York Times,</u> March 11, 2018

Chapter 5: Islam and Extremism

1   This quotation is taken from the internet website: www.thinkexist.com.

2   https://www.merriam-webster.com/dictionary/extremism

3   https://www.brainyquote.com/quotes/bertrand_russell_408841

4   This quotation is taken from the internet website: www.thinkexist.com.

5   http://www.azquotes.com/author/2886-Winston_Churchill/tag/socialism

6   This article was published on September 16, 2012. It was taken from the internet website link: http://www.psychologytoday.com/blog/21st-century-aging/201209/differences-between-men-and-women

7   Ibid

8   This quote is taken from the internet website: thinkexist.com.

9   Adeel Zeerak, <u>Women, Feminism, and Islam</u>, (USA: Createspace, 2014). This book is available at www.Amazon.com.

10   Paul A. Samuelson and William D. Nordhaus, <u>Economics</u>, 14th edition (McGraw-Hill Inc., 1992), p. 21.

11   Mufti Muhammad Taqi Usmani, <u>An introduction to Islamic Finance</u>, (Karachi: Maktaba Ma'ariful Quran, 2002), p. 17 – 18.

12   Broadcast to the people of Australia, 19 February 1948.

13   Dr. Lothrop Stoddard, <u>The New World of Islam</u>, (London: 1932)

14   Maurice Bucaille, <u>The Bible, The Qur'an and Science</u>. This book is available at the internet website:
http://archive.org/details/TheBibletheQuranScienceByDr.mauriceBucaille

15   Marmaduke Picktall, <u>Islamic Culture</u>, p. 67 - 68.

16   Nick Higham and Margaret Ryan, <u>BBC</u>, 21 January 2012.
(http://news.bbc.co.uk/2/hi/uk_news/8472111.stm)

17   Marquis of Dufferin and Ava, Speeches delivered in India, (London: 1890), p. 24.

Chapter 6: Islam and Non-Muslims

1   Quoted in The Great Arab Conquests, from Tarikh Tabari.
http://lostislamichistory.com/jerusalem-and-umar-ibn-al-khattab/

2   Michael Hart, <u>The 100: A ranking of the most influential persons in history</u>, (Great Britain: Simon & Schuster Ltd, 1992), p. 265.

3   De Lacy O'Leary, <u>Islam at the Crossroads,</u> (London: 1923), p. 8.

4   https://yaqeeninstitute.org/en/tesneem-alkiek/religious-minorities/

5   Qaradawi, Yusuf, '<u>al-Aqaliyyat ad-Diniyya wa-Hal al-Islami,</u>' p. 58-59

6   "Muslim boys up late for Ramadan saved lives by knocking on peoples' doors when fire broke out during Grenfell Tower blaze," <u>Mirror,</u> June 15, 2017.

(http://www.mirror.co.uk/news/uk-news/muslims-up-late-ramadan-fire-10620514)

7   https://www.launchgood.com/project/muslims_united_for_las_vegas_victims#!/

8   Melissa Chan, "Forgotten stories of Muslims who saved Jewish people during the holocaust," <u>TIME,</u> January 27, 2017

(http://time.com/4651298/holocaust-memorial-day-muslims-jews/)

9   https://www.jewishbookcouncil.org/book/the-grand-mosque-of-paris-a-story-of-how-muslims-saved-jews-during-the-holocaust

10   http://www.nkusa.org/AboutUs/Zionism/opposition.cfm

Chapter 7: The Concept of Jihad

1   This quotation is taken from the internet website: www.thinkexist.com.

2   Muqaddimaat, Ibn Rushd, known in the Western world as Averroes, p. 259.

3 http://www.aboutjihad.com/terrorism/islam_jihad_terrorism.php

4 Dr. Israr Ahmed, <u>Jihad Fi Sabee Lillah,</u> (Lahore: Nazim Maktaba Markazi Anjuman-i-Khuddam-ul-Quran, 2000).

5 https://www.brainyquote.com/quotes/albert_einstein_143096

6 Researchers of Islamic Research Institute, International Islamic University Islamabad, <u>Paigham-i-Pakistan,</u> (Islamabad: Islamic Research Institute, 2018).

7 Ibid, pp. 34 – 36

8 Ibid, pp. 36 - 37

9 Ibid, pp. 30 - 31

10 Ben Dupre, <u>50 Political Ideas you really need to know,</u> Quercus, London, 2010, pp. 180.

11 Chris Hedges, "What every person should know about war," <u>The New York Times,</u> July 6, 2003

(http://www.nytimes.com/2003/07/06/books/chapters/what-every-person-should-know-about-war.html)

CONCLUDING REMARKS:

1 This quotation is taken from the internet website: www.brainyquote.com.

APPENDIX: ISLAM A RELIGION OF PEACE?

1
http://materiaislamica.com/index.php/2013_Oxford_University_Debate:_Is_Islam_a_Religion_of_Peace%3F_(Mehdi_Hassan%27s_Passionate_and_Wi
nning_Speech_on_the_Defence_of_Islam_and_Muslims)

Adeel Zeerak

(https://www.youtube.com/watch?v=Jy9tNyp03M0)

INDEX

7/7, 12, 15, 39, 49, 140, 144

9/11, 9, 10, 12, 14, 15, 16, 18, 20, 24, 27, 30, 33, 39, 49, 65, 67, 68, 69, 72, 80, 143, 148

Abortion, 28, 142

Abu Bakr, 96, 97

Abu Bakr al-Baghdadi, 54

Adultery, 45

Afghanistan, 9, 15, 17, 18, 36, 56, 57, 58, 67, 69, 71

AIDS, 123

Agencies/Agency, 11, 12, 28, 34, 36, 37, 38, 55, 57, 58, 69, 75

Aggression, 101, 104, 109, 119, 122, 124, 133, 135, 146

Algeria, 65, 109

Ali, 45, 89, 97, 102, 131

Alienation, 65

Alim, 47, 54

Allah, 12, 41, 44, 45, 47, 50, 52, 53, 54, 55, 60, 82, 83, 84, 85, 86, 87, 88, 89, 98, 100, 102, 103, 113, 118, 119, 121

Allegation, 45

Allies, 9, 10, 14, 109

Al-Qaeda, 69, 70, 143

Ambassador, 66, 140

America, 52, 66, 142

Amil Kumar Gupta, 38

Ammunition, 26

Amnesty, 125

Anarchist, 18

Angel, 11, 45

Animal, 61

Anti-Sematic, 107, 108

Apostasy, 45

Arab, 18, 65, 66, 108, 109, 126, 228, 133

Arabic, 12, 44, 61, 71, 93, 112, 118, 143

Armed, 18, 22, 25, 33, 36, 48, 66, 71, 113, 114, 117, 119, 124

Armor, 102

Army, 28, 36, 40, 56, 57, 58, 103, 105, 119, 130, 142

Army of God, 11, 28

Arson, 25, 61, 142

Ascetic, 82

Asia, 69, 104

Assassination, 31

Astronomy, 93

Atheist, 142, 145

Atrocities/Atrocity, 15, 123, 124

Attack, 9, 14, 17, 27, 28, 30, 40, 50, 52, 53, 62, 76, 101, 103, 120, 131

Authority, 88, 89, 120

Baghdad, 17, 54, 70, 93

ABOUT THE AUTHOR

Adeel Zeerak was born on December 9, 1968, in Karachi, a sprawling, cosmopolitan city and the business hub of Pakistan. He received his early education at the local Christian missionary schools in Karachi. He then joined D J Science College in Karachi to receive his 'intermediate' college education. He graduated with a Mechanical Engineering degree from NED University of Engineering and Technology, Karachi, Pakistan, in 1993. He did his Masters in Business Administration (MBA) with a dual-specialization in Marketing and Finance from the Institute of Business Administration (IBA), Karachi, Pakistan, in 1999. Adeel Zeerak is also a 'Certified Supply Chain Professional' (CSCP) from APICS, USA. In addition he has attended numerous management and technical trainings including a four-week training held in Malaysia on 'Workshop on Green-Productivity for trainers and consultants'. The training was sponsored by the Asian Productivity Organization, Tokyo, Japan. Adeel Zeerak has also successfully completed an 84-hour online training on 'Politics, Media and War: 9/11 and its aftermaths' from The Open University, UK.

While working as a management consultant at the Pakistan Institute of Management (PIM), Adeel Zeerak has developed and conducted various trainings throughout Pakistan predominantly in the fields of General Management and Operations Management. He has also been involved in conducting trainings arranged by UNDP in collaboration with the Sindh Government for planning officers on the topic of 'Gender Sensitive Project Planning Skills'. These trainings were part of a joint venture project between UNDP and the Government of Pakistan by the name of 'Gender Based Governance Systems (GBG).'

Adeel Zeerak has also served the manufacturing sector of Pakistan in various capacities for almost 13 years. During this period, he was mainly involved with the automotive sector.

Adeel Zeerak's study in Islam includes attending a 'Fahm-i-Deen' course by Idara Taleemat-i-Deenya, Jamia Madina Jadeed, Lahore, Pakistan. The course, with a proposed duration of one year, is developed by Dr. Mufti Abdul Wahid of Jamia Madina Jadeed, Lahore, Pakistan.

Adeel Zeerak studied this course under the guidance of Maulana Abbus Sattar at Baitus Salam Masjid, Karachi, Pakistan.

He has also attended a three months course on the 'Basic themes of Islam' organized by Anjuman Khuddam-ul-Quran Sindh, Karachi, Pakistan. This organization was founded by Dr. Israr Ahmed, a renowned Islamic scholar from Pakistan. Adeel Zeerak has also attended a one-month Islamic Course organized by Sirat-i-Mustaqim Foundation, Karachi, Pakistan. The course was designed and administered under the supervision of Dr. Ghulam Murtaza Malik, who was also a renowned Islamic scholar from Pakistan.

In addition to the above mentioned formal trainings on Islam, Adeel Zeerak discovered a lot about Islam by reading the books or listening to the lectures of various traditional Ulema including Mufti Muhammad Taqi Usmani, Mufti Rafi Usmani, Mufti Muhammad Shafi, Dr. Mufti Abdul Wahid, Maulana Syed Abul Hassan Ali Nadawi, Maulana Yousuf Ludhyanv, Mufti Nazeer Ahmed and Maulana Engineer Asad-ur-Rehman. Adeel Zeerak has also read many books or listened to the lectures of many other Islamic scholars like Maulana Abul Aala Maududi, Dr. Israr Ahmed, Dr. Ghulam Murtaza Malik, Professor Khursheed Ahmed, Dr. Zakir Naik, Mr. Adnan Oktar (pen-name: Harun Yahya), and Mr. Shujauddin Shaikh.

Adeel Zeerak is also a great admirer of Martial Arts. He is himself a Black Belt holder of the world renowned Japanese martial art of Shotokan Karate. His other hobbies include swimming and reading. He maintains a personal library with a collection on various topics including Engineering, Medical and General Sciences, Management, Economics, Finance, Martial Arts, Mathematics, History, and Islam.